Tom Fischer 3-15-94

Uncertain Seasons

Uncertain Seasons

Elizabeth Shelfer Morgan

THE UNIVERSITY OF ALABAMA PRESS
TUSCALOOSA & LONDON

∞

The paper on which this book is printed meets the minimum
requirements of American National Standard for Information
Science-Permanence of Paper for Printed Library Materials,
ANSI Z39.48-1984.

Library of Congress Cataloging-in-Publication Data

Morgan, Elizabeth Shelfer, 1938–
Uncertain seasons / Elizabeth Shelfer Morgan.

p. cm.

The text is interspersed with transcriptions of letters to members of
the author's family from William Howard Shelfer ("Uncle Howard").

ISBN 0-8173-0702-8 (alk. paper)

1. Morgan, Elizabeth Shelfer, 1938–   2. World War, 1939–1945—
Florida—Havana.   3. Havana (Fla.)—Social life and customs.

4. World War, 1939–1945—Personal narratives, American.

5. Children—Florida—Havana—Biography.

6. Shelfer, William Howard, d. 1944—Correspondence.

7. Soldier—United States—Correspondence.

8. United States.   Army—Biography.

I. Shelfer, William Howard, d. 1944. II. Title.

D769.85.F6H386   1994

975.9'925—dc20   93-18428

British Library Cataloguing-in-Publication Data available

For
my husband, Mark

and
our grown children
Amy Elizabeth
George Cass
Allison Stacy
Charles Howard

Contents

Preface

For as long as I can remember, I knew I would tell my story.

It is the story of a past when family and neighbors had time for each other and each other's children, when schools and churches operated with combined resources, when men, women, and children went about their work and war and life with pride and a noble acceptance. Without this account neither my children nor my younger brother, Richard, born in 1949, would know of those who nurtured me. My extended family included not only my kin, but also my teachers, people of the community, and the mothers, fathers, brothers, and sisters of all my friends. My story is patterned after my beloved hometown of Havana, Florida, and the letters are the words of my uncle, 1st Lt. William Howard Shelfer.

The childhood narrative is a dreamlike recollection the way memory works and is not a family history nor a researched volume of documentation. For this reason, I do not use the Shelfer name. Because I needed to distance myself from the emotion I experienced each day that I wrote and each time I saw my name in the letters, I chose part of my sister's name, Sara Ruth.

Reading the letters and opening my uncle's trunk for the first time, I became a young girl again recalling scenes and sensations as I had perceived them at that time. Why some events and long-ago acquaintances stand out more than others, I do not know. I only know what came to me as I continued to read the letters, finally touching his books, his clothes, his insignia. I found his scroll-like, handwritten copy of *The Rubaiyat of Omar Khayyam* and was immediately reminded of the rolled-up recital pieces I had often clutched before a performance, hoping to absorb the contents for reassurance and comfort.

It is not my intention to omit anyone. There are those dear to me whose influence I received at another time in my life.

Most of the names and sequences of events have been changed. Portions of some letters have been combined to prevent repetition. Except for phonetically spelled locations, which were corrected, my given name, which was changed to Sari, and my family name, which was changed to Bradford, the letters are unedited and are the source of my remembrance.

For many reasons, I thank my husband, Mark, who has encouraged me in anything I have ever wanted to do. I am also indebted to Dr. Sheila Ortiz Taylor, Florida State University Creative Writing Professor, who helped me find a way to tell my story, and Dr. William Warren Rogers, Professor of History, Florida State University, who since its inception would not let me put the manuscript aside and recommended it to his publisher.

E.S.M.

Uncertain
Seasons

1

A Time to Every Purpose

"Well, Sari, Howard bought my lunch today," said Mama. Her words are so predictable around the first of every month, that I can form them without even listening to her. She always says them as if she had been escorted to lunch by the most sought-after, best-dressed young gentleman at the community dance. Of course, I know that she means the $4.26 government check is still enough to pay for the vegetable plate at Morrison's. I close my eyes and see the little brown envelope stamped Official Business, the greenish blue insurance check inside, and think how much that small amount of money continues to represent—remaining a gentle reminder of my own simple childhood unknowingly protected from the shadow of a more complex adult world making history around me.

I don't know if my early memory is my own recollection or if the stories told to me or around me have so stamped my mind with people and events that my participation seems more like sleepwalking. When I try to remember, I see only fragments of rooms, some recognizable, some not, with people in them speaking in unfinished sentences: time fragments, moving fast and then slow—belonging to uncertain seasons, uncertain years. When I look back, so many times I feel I was on the outside looking in on the life I was supposed to be living, not knowing whether I visited the backyards of the years through the mind's eye of my Granddaddy or whether I walked among them holding his hand.

Back then, time was measured by the seasons. The weather, that culprit or creator of crops and adventure, was at the center of intimacy among hunters and fishermen, mostly farmers by occupation. These people, my people, didn't just pass the time of day discussing the weather. They speculated about it, prayed about it, feared it, shared it, and held it sacred. Events were recalled by the kind of day it had been.

Take the cold February night the house burned in 1936 when I, along with one bureau drawer of my clothes, was taken next door to stay with Cousin Sadie. Someone jerked me from the safe sleep of my warm bed to the neighboring screened porch, which became my observation post. I don't remember hearing shots my Daddy fired to alert the volunteer firemen, but his story became a favorite among the old-timers sitting on the town benches:

"That Dink went outside and shot his gun, put it back in his closet and let it burn up with his house."

The year we lived with relatives while the house was being rebuilt remains a blurry kaleidoscope of scenes that change with the slightest flash of memory, never to be recaptured quite the same again. It seems there were rows of beds on a sleeping porch from where I watched charred sticks come falling down. I sometimes tiptoed among blackened mason jars and bedsprings. When we moved back home, people had been shifted all around. Granddaddy still had his room and Uncle Howard his, but my new baby sister had my baby bed. Because the upstairs rooms were not there as before, Aunt Mable Miller, "Mamie" as everybody called her, and her family now had a house next door. Her two grown children, Helen and Jim, were away at college most of the time. Mamie, Daddy's sister, was the one in the family who kept the important papers and the book we all signed at Thanksgiving. She was also my second grade teacher.

"Sari, take this reading book and sit in the hall and listen to Curtis read until the bell rings."

"But Aunt Mamie, I . . ."

"Curtis, get a desk from the seventh grade homeroom and pay attention when Sari helps you."

Curtis Pippin sat in the big desk and I in one of the smaller chairs I used from my own reading group, the bluebirds. He was so much older and bigger than the rest of the boys in my class. I felt sorry for him, but at the same time, I was scared to be alone with him in the hall. Curtis went barefooted in the summer and when it was cold wore laced-up boots bordered with red clay. The only place I kept my eyes was on the book in my hand—his he kept on the dirty fingernail he used to trace the words underneath the pictures as he read,

"Come and play!"

"Come and play!"

"Jump, Puppy, jump!"

"Jump, Little Puppy, jump!"

He could pronounce the words right when the pictures were there.

I was quickly becoming Aunt Mamie's assistant. Not only did she run the grammar school, she costumed the Christmas pageant and organized and narrated the annual May Day program. She counted on me to help out and fill in anywhere, and without practice.

"Sari, one of the fourth graders is sick. I know you'll fit into her dress. You can put your hair up in pin curls under the rabbit hat you're wearing as Peter Cottontail's mother, then change in time for the Maypole Dance."

The high school band played "Pomp and Circumstance" as the May Queen and her court slowly marched the entire length of the softball field. The girls wore long pastel evening dresses and were escorted by their fellow classmates in dinner jackets. They watched Mamie's program put on in their honor—the Senior Class of 1941.

First grade girls dressed in pansy, zinnia, and daffodil bonnets of crepe paper skipped and performed in their dark green to "Dance of the Flowers."

As I changed into my light blue organdy dress and brushed my hair, I looked out the bathroom transom and caught the end of the third graders' act. Their wooden-hinged toy movements were believable as they exaggerated every step and jerk of their arms to the band's rendition of "Wedding of the Painted Dolls." Each spit curl was in place on their white-powdered faces—their cheeks round circles of pink rouge. The girls' brows and the boys' mustaches were so heavily penciled that they looked like caricatures of Nelson Eddy and Jeanette McDonald posing on the front of Aunt Mamie's sheet music.

It was time for the big finale, and I was there holding a smooth satin streamer doing my part to weave in among the other colored ribbons attached to the tall white may-pole.

Even though Aunt Mamie was good at directing people, her real calling was directing music. For years she had led the singing in the school auditorium as conscientiously as she directed the Methodist Church choir. Every Friday at chapel she led the entire student body in lively renditions of songs such as:

> Reuben, Reuben, I've been thinking
> What a Grand Life this would be
> If the boys were all transported
> Far across the big, blue sea.

And transported they soon were—boys and men in uniform and my twenty-three-year-old Uncle Howard among them.

That spring he left for Camp Blanding. It was a little after Valentine's Day. I know it was around that time because I had just thrown away Fletcher Link's dead flower. For all the girls in our class, his mother always made big red construction paper valentines with a big pink camellia in the center tied in place with a white ribbon. She would bring them to our classroom on a tray.

February 25, 1941
Camp Blanding, Florida

Dear Dad:

I passed the physical exams with no trouble at all. The doctors say that there is nothing wrong with my heart. I have been stationed in the infantry.

It has been a hard week, they started me out with a twenty eight pound pack the first thing but I got along very well. We march seven miles each day. The miles are going to and from the woods that we train in. I have dug holes, jumped in them and pretended to shoot, then got out and covered the hole up again. Running through the woods with that pack and falling on your belly is no picnic.

I have been lucky that I have no blisters on my feet; most of the boys have them. While marching out yesterday after dinner, four men out of our company fell out. The weather was pretty hot. It is a surprise to me, but I can stand the running as good or better than most of these boys.

I started to call you up this evening and I would have if I

thought that Sari would be close by to talk over the phone. I
sure do miss her. Give my love to all,

I am your son,

No. 34023684

Private William H. Bradford

A. P. B. 31-31 Division

Co. "I" 115 Inf.

Camp Blanding, Florida

For most of that year things stayed pretty much the same around Richland, our little North Florida town of about 1,000. Richland is located in the upper part of the state close to where the Gulf of Mexico has taken a little chomp out of the curve called the Big Bend. We are five miles south of the Georgia line and the sign south on the main highway reads, "Tallahassee, 16 miles." The Apalachicola River borders our county of Gadsden on the west. The Ochlockonee River is the eastern boundary and about five miles or twenty-five minutes away from our house by way of Granddaddy's car. You had to allow for him to stop, get out, and meander up and down the dirt road looking for turkey tracks.

The land was the mainstay here, and planting went on as usual with each change of the seasons. Around midwinter the farmers cultivated their seed beds anticipating another thriving tobacco crop. Grandaddy would say, "The quality of what you raise depends mostly on the kind of soil you plant it in." I couldn't help but feel he meant children as well as crops. Our county's subsoil of red clay with no presence of rotten limestone and the perfect climate provided just the right spot for growing shade tobacco—brown gold, our first big industry.

The farmers waited for the first good rain shower around the middle of April, then the farm labor moved the plants from the smaller beds and set them out in larger fields, which sometimes covered as many as thirty to forty acres. When Granddaddy first took me inside a tobacco shade and I saw how necessary every worker was to keeping the crop underway, I knew then where the term "hands" must have come from. A homemade wooden tool resembling an oversized, sawed-off dinner fork was used for making holes in the rows of dirt. Colored women dressed in overcoats with felt hats sometimes over their headrags, dropped the tender plants from their baskets next to these holes. Young laborers who could squat, bend, and almost stand on their heads all day secured the plants in place in their special holes. Children carried buckets of water for an older worker who watered each plant with a dipper fashioned from a tin can attached to a long thin wooden slat. This transplanting was done at intervals up until the first of May in case of a late frost. It was foolish and downright dangerous to transplant much later since harvesting would begin in late May when school was out.

༺

We were busy at work during recess—reshaping our established playhouse, its walls defined and lined with short twigs and pine straw. It looked like a big game of hopscotch except each block of outlined room had a little opening for a door. We had taken care to build it all under a low-hanging, leafy hickory branch for shade.

Mary Jean was sweeping the dirt floor with the make-shift broom of dried bushes. Patsy sat on top of a wooden drink crate while I began plumping the nests of oak leaves we used for our dolls' beds. Sally stirred the acorns in the jar-top lids we used for pans simmering on top of our stove, a big chunky piece of concrete we had found in the ditch.

The boys gathered ammunition for their continual pine cone war. Dirt flew from the deep hole One Side was digging. It now held three soldiers. Poles were lying across the ditch, and most of the Other Side was repairing their stick hideout—weaving the limbs like latticework and covering them again in pine straw and magnolia leaves the wind had blown away.

I had just finished my apple, when I saw Aunt Mamie coming toward the playground. Vester Pierce, Hall Monitor, was with her carrying the dreaded dodge ball—that hollow, rust-colored rubber ball that bounced higher than your head and had a plinky, tinlike sound when it hit you in the back or vibrated on the hard-packed red clay.

The fun came to a halt. Even though it was the last day of school, we must play the organized game. So we left our dolls, and the boys put down their wooden guns.

May 29, 1941

Camp Blanding, Florida

Dear Dink,

This past week, I have carried my rifle about 50 miles and sometimes I think it is a better man than I am. In the afternoon, it feels like a piece of railroad iron. We may go out on the range to shoot next week. I sure do want to shoot the damn thing.

Most of the boys are gone on passes and the camp is practically deserted. I went to the theater this evening. It is in the big tent you saw. I will try to come home next weekend. Don't count on it too strong for there is a chance Uncle Sam may change my mind.

Your brother,

Howard

There was a chance there was going to be something way out of the ordinary that June. I might see my very first movie star in person.

We stopped by the ice plant like always on the way to Wakulla Springs—we went two or three times during the summer on Sunday afternoons. Mr. Munley slowly got up from the ladder-back chair he sat in tilted back against the wall. He disappeared into the walk-in icebox, finally reappearing and walking across the wooden platform. In his hand he held an oversized pair of black tongs that clutched our big block of ice. He plopped it down in the washtub next to the watermelon and jars of tea and potato salad. Ruthie and I sat on quilts in the back of the dairy truck next to the basket of fried chicken and Mama's cake saver.

"We may get to see Johnny Weismuller, the real Tarzan," I told Ruthie. "Don't let his ape call scare you."

"Remember Cheetah?"

"Cheetah, Cheetah, red-bug eater."

"Cheater, Cheater, red-bug eater," we both chanted over and over again.

It made sense that the Tarzan movies could be made at Wakulla Springs. It was one of the world's deepest freshwater springs and known for its underwater caves. The water was so crystal clear you could see fish swimming among the tall grass that bordered the area where we swam, that is, if we could stand the icy water. You had to take a deep breath and jump right in or go underwater and stay there or you'd freeze to death. Daddy always made us come out when our lips turned blue. The swimming area, including the three-story diving tower and several painted barges for sunbathing, gave way to the river, a safe distance away, filled with water lilies, turtles, and alligators. The banks of the river were a tangled mess of trees and vines, a perfect jungle for the treehouse of Tarzan and Jane. Near the picnic area, Daddy pointed out a kind of float stored there which the cameramen used for underwater scenes, but there were no movie stars to be seen.

We dressed at the bathhouse, and before we loaded up for home we watched the teenagers jitterbugging in their bathing suits on the concrete floor of the open pavilion— a concession stand on one side, juke box on the other.

On the way home I had unbelievable visions of sunken treasure inside the underwater cave; its entry I had seen 120 feet down from the glass-bottom boats at one time or another. I couldn't say I was really too disappointed that we didn't at least spot Tarzan somewhere. After all, I was there, there at the very scene I might later recognize at the afternoon picture show.

I watched the palmettos flash by and thought how I would ride over this same road in the fall when we made the trip to the bay for the salt fish. Just as sure as mullet spawning time rolled around after the last full moon in October, Daddy and Granddaddy would load the old stone crock and head toward Shell Point. They had the mullet dressed and covered with salt—the coarse, chunky kind. We would have all the salt fish and roe we could eat for breakfast during the fall and winter. I didn't know it then, but that trip to the coast would be our last anywhere for a while.

෴

It was along about the beginning of Lightning Bug season of the next year when we began to get letters from Ft. Benning, Georgia. Uncle Howard enrolled in Officer's Candidate School and from there promised to send me a pink organdy dress and a pair of black, patent-leather shoes. Now centered in the glass portion of our front door was the big, white star decal bordered in blue framed by the crocheted panel behind. This star emblem marked our house as the home of a serviceman willing and able to give his life for his country.

May 5, 1942

Dear Dad,

First I will tell you that this is a touch. I am going to do what I have always done when I needed some things, ask you for them. I will get to that a little later.

About a month ago I was called before a board of officers for an interview. This took place at the Infantry School on the main post here at Benning. I went over with a very high recommendation from Captain Walker. As a result of the interview, the officers rate you and classify you according to that rating. If you make a good rating, you will be called to the school before someone that made a poorer rating, even if he was examined before you were.

You will be pleased to know that I made a very good showing for when the decision from the board came to my outfit, there was an order to prepare me for transfer as quickly as possible. The order came in last Thursday at noon. As a result of that, I attended a class that same afternoon. I am now a candidate in the Officer's Training School. My class, which is a company of 210 men, will graduate on the 26th of July.

It is customary for a person to get a five day pass between the time he gets his notice to report to the school and that time. In my case there was no time, so I got no time off. I don't mind so much although I would like to have seen you all before I started this course. This is a hard three months. I am very glad now that I have had good training. It will be easier for me than some of the men here.

To get back to the main part of this letter. The reason I need some money is this school has forced me to buy some clothes. I bought and paid for two summer uniforms and a small foot locker or trunk. I had to pay for this stuff and luckily I had the money, but I have other obligations. To make it short, I need $20.00 by the 15th of this month. I could get the money if I were back in K Co., but here I am among strangers. If you can help here, good. If you can't, please write right away and let me know.

The men I am with here are all fine men, most of them have a good bit of schooling. I wish you could see the way I have to keep my room. There is a prescribed way for everything. If you could come up some Sunday, I would be easy to find. Anyone in town (it is about the size of Richland) could tell you where I live.

I have some lessons to prepare. Please let me hear soon.

Give my love to all,
Howard

Some of the letters were passed among family members. Only portions of them were read aloud—sometimes a few lines to Ruthie and me if he sent us a special message. When I thought of Uncle Howard after he first left, I pictured him running up the front walk stepping on Mama's periwinkles and later with my new pink dress over his shoulder, but as time passed and he didn't get any more furloughs, I mostly remembered the cigar smell of his clothes.

June 11, 1942

Dear Dink,

I have really been busy. From 5:30 A.M. on Monday to 4:30 on Saturday, I do not have a minute of spare time. This course is only 90 days and there is a lot to be covered. I am through with studying the weapons. I qualified as a expert with all of the weapons used in the Infantry with the exception of the hand grenade. We are studying tactics now and it is more interesting than the first few weeks have been.

Being here is a hell of a strain on a man. We are watched all of the time. We know that there will be about 20% of the class to fail to graduate. The men who do not get their commission will be made a Sgt. of the first grade. I don't believe I have anything to worry about. I seem to be getting along alright. When we graduate we will get $150.00 along with our commission. That is to help buy clothes.

This is the first Sunday I have spent in camp in some time. I am confined as a result of gambling in the barracks. Gambling is something that is unbecoming to an officer and a gentleman. The thing that is bad about it, is getting caught.

I wish you could see me graduate. There won't be much of a ceremony, but it is a big thing to me. The biggest thing that could happen.

They are really putting pressure on us now. When I get out of here I am really going to need a rest. Three months here, if you take it seriously, is Hell on a man.

I am trying to get all I can out of the school for I feel that I will be dealing with human lives very shortly. It will be little short of a crime if I don't get all I can from these three months.

It is a pity that wife of yours can't see my quarters. Everything is in its place all of the time. I don't only make up my bed, but sweep and mop under it each morning. If we do anything wrong, like leaving a wrinkle in the bed (a very little wrinkle) we get a demerit. Too many of these demerits and I won't get a Commission at the end of the course. It would break my heart to fail.

I guess you are wondering about this stationery with the wide lines. The school gives it to us to work field problems. It comes out of a writing tablet.

I have some lessons to prepare. At present we are studying map reading. I am going to stop now and shine my shoes so that I won't be in a rush tomorrow morning.

> Your brother,
> Candidate William H. Bradford
> Co. 11 34d Student Training
> Reg. I. S. S. C.
> Ft. Benning, Ga. O.C.

P.S. If it won't be too much trouble, I would like to have some tobacco—some black and strong.

❧

The cool, amber-colored water of Roady's Creek tingled our bare legs as we waded in. We didn't go all the way up to our shorts because the cola-colored water hid the holes and roots we knew were there. Sally was the first to head back for the bicycles we had left by the road.

"Come on," she called. "Let's hurry. Mr. Charlie will be wondering what happened to us."

"If we eat as soon as we get there, we'll have plenty of time to play," said Mary Jean.

We rode caravan style—three different hues and stages of Toni Home Permanents outlined against the July haze. Each head was adorned with curl loosening at its own "Summer Vacation," three month's pace becoming "just right" for the first day of school. Our threesome made this dirt-road outing most every Saturday that summer when I was eight. I say "dirt-road" because few outside of the city limits were paved. We often stopped a while, kicked up the sand with our bare feet, or dug our big toes in the packed coolness of the ditches as we picked wildflowers.

I could see the black '40 Ford parked under the huge oak trees next to the cemetery. I knew Granddaddy was sitting in the driver's seat waiting—and nodding. The faded green straw basket would be next to him; the basket so loosely woven that the food placed inside formed its shape, bulging here, sucked in there. Mama would have made the pimento cheese sandwiches and my favorite— peanut butter and fig preserves. The bananas would be there; bananas he called ripe and we called rotten. The chocolate-covered creams in the no-brand cellophane bag always served as our dessert.

We sat under one of the huge oaks on an old blanket Granddaddy always kept in the trunk of his car. Bradford cemetery was on a little knoll about one and a half miles east of Richland. From where we were sitting, it was possible to make out the rectangular tobacco fields covered with cheesecloth. I leaned against the tree and smelled the fruity scent of somebody's freshly mown grass mixed with the Prince Albert smoke now coming from Granddaddy's pipe. He felt obliged to give us the same information over and over again any time we were near the tobacco farms. He recited it like a poem that didn't rhyme.

"You know," he continued puffing on his pipe, "this spot right here in North Florida is the only place, 'cept for Connecticut, where they grow tobacco under a shade." We listened politely as we finished sipping iced tea from our jars.

"See here, those barns down yonder are full right now with green tobacco hanging from the rafters. Somebody's inside there tending the fires that'll turn those leaves into dry, thin, yellowgold. Yes sir, those leaves will be used as the outside wrapper for some bully good cigars."

"I'll race you to the spigot," said Sally. After eating the sweet sandwiches, our hands were plenty sticky. It was a relief to rinse and dry them on our shirttails.

Granddaddy joined us as we walked together toward the squeaky gate. It was waist high like a garden gate except it was black wrought iron—with spikes on top. On the front was a small plaque shaped like a coat of arms with the words, "Stewart Iron Works, Cincinnati, Ohio." The graveyard was completely enclosed with the spiky iron fence Daddy and Uncle Howard had put up when they were only young boys.

We walked reverently among the graves in the cemetery my great-great-grandfather had started years ago.

Granddaddy commented about the life and death represented by each tombstone as we read the inscriptions:
"FOR GOD SO LOVED THE WORLD"
"Cliff's twins, died of diphtheria in 1907," he said.
"VALIANT SOLDIER"
"Roscoe's boy killed in World War I."
A headstone built for two—the empty space by Granddaddy's Eva.
"SHE HATH DONE WHAT SHE COULD"
"That's my place," he said.
Satisfied with his nostalgic and historical contribution, Granddaddy put out his pipe, and as he fanned himself with his crinkled straw hat, went back to the car for a nap. He was in no hurry. "In no hurry a'tall," he'd say. He had time to take me and my friends anywhere we needed or wanted to go. He took us uptown when it was cold, to school when it rained, to medicine shows, to cane grindings, to the Saturday afternoon picture show, and even all the way to Panacea to the fishing lodge belonging to Uncle Elbert, Grandaddy's brother. On the way, Granddaddy always insisted we stop at that spring and drink some of the healthy, stinking sulphur water.

Sally and Mary Jean were already stretched out on the cool, marble slabs taking the Dracula positions and pretending to be ghosts of the dead.

"So this time I'm the one who's lost in the cemetery at night?" I asked. They didn't answer and I knew that was my signal to hide among the stones in silence until their stiff, calculated steps and outstretched arms found me. I worried as I waited there about disturbing the sleep of the dead. I knew we all felt a little ashamed for running and stepping on hallowed ground, but it was *my* family cemetery, and, unless there was a funeral, even Brother Kittle had no business here.

I could hear them coming as I crouched closer—my face pressed against the cool marble. I had been in one position behind the stone for quite a while, and I finally had to shift my leg, which had gone to sleep. Quickly, I steadied myself by encircling my arm around the upright stone. Instantly my fingers touched the outline of the crossed rifles. A soldier's stone.

"Gotcha," they said in unison.

July 8, 1942

Dear Sister-in-law,

This afternoon I am uncommonly happy because I just got a letter from my old sister-in-law. Lib, you will never know how much I would like for you to sweep under my feet again. Do you remember what a time you had waiting on me and how I rested before I left. I bet now you are sorry you hid my cigars. It is funny how things come to mind. I well remember the first time Dink and I first saw you. You were standing in the door the day we came after the goat. That goat sure was a tool of fate. You see, if it was not for me (and the goat) you may not have the little girls I love so much. The word of this is—keep on being good to your brother-in-law. You know how puny I was before you brought me out of the kinks.

Well, this will be all for the time being, but don't forget

that you are my favorite sister-in-law and I can promise you
that I ain't gonna forget it. In a few weeks I hope to be able
to send home a money order for you to buy yourself and
your daughters something. Did Dad get my letter?

> With love to all,
> The best brother-in-law you got,
> Howard

Uncle Howard had been almost thirteen when his mother died, and I guess all the family thought he needed something to take his mind off things. So he and Daddy built a cart and went looking for a goat to pull it. Granddaddy always said that "Daddy found the girl and Uncle Howard got the goat."

After the postcard saying he had arrived in North Carolina, Uncle Howard wrote first to Daddy.

> Ft. Bragg, N.C.
> August 7, 1942
> 2035

Dear Dink,

That big number on the right is the way we keep time in
the army. To translate that for you, it is 8:35. Honestly, I don't
have much time to write. Besides my duty with the troops as
a Platoon Commander, I am supply officer and that has
worked me overtime. I work at least 14 hours each day. I
only regret that I cannot work more. I like my work and am
doing my very best. Please tell Dad and explain it to him that

I don't like for him to tell in his letters for me to try and be an instructor and stay in the good old U.S.A. In every letter he mentions that. My sole purpose here is to serve where I am needed. There are people here to decide when and where that will be.

Remember that I am very glad to hear from home.

With love to all,
Your brother,
Howard, 2nd Lt.

One hot evening that same year when it was almost time for school to start again, the whole family was sitting on the porch like we always did after supper. Aunt Mamie had already been in Granddaddy's room earlier that day with the door shut. Because she was here again, sitting with Mama, Daddy, and Granddaddy on the porch, I knew that they were all discussing some pretty important business. Ruthie and I tried to listen from the swing on the other end of the long, wraparound porch, but we could only make out a few phrases. They rocked back and forth in the rocking chairs talking in low murmurs. Their voices rose and then hushed like Daddy's smoke rings—sometimes hanging there and clear, then becoming distorted and quickly dissolving.

From what we could piece together, it seems Uncle Howard married someone named Eileen Turtlelow, from way down in Miami. She was a girl he had met while he was stationed at Camp Blanding near Tampa, and soon he would most certainly be sent overseas.

August 18, 1942

Dear Dad and Dink:

Thanks very much for sending the clothes. If you have not already sent the other things, please don't. Give the whole mess away except the shirts—that means shoes, raincoat, and anything else that I may have left behind. Save the wool shirts.

We have received our mission and now are making last minute preparations.

We are amphibious troops—something like the marines. We are trained to fight on land and water. The nature of our training is to hit the beach in small boats and hit the beach fighting. Each boat has in it a complete fighting team. After we have fought our way inland to a designated spot, we re-organize back into our own outfits. There is a lake here that we have been practicing on. About every afternoon we have a landing operation. I am glad I have a good knowledge of all the weapons, because we have some of them all in each boat. We have everything crated up and marked N.Y.P.E., meaning New York, Point of Embarkation. That, of course, is the only address I know. I am looking forward to the future as being a great adventure. It is a big thing and while it is going to be horrible, it will at the same time be very exciting.

My company commander says that I am due for a promotion soon. I hope I get it before we leave as there are no promotions made while in combat.

As you know, an officer does not carry a pack, his bedroll and tent are carried on a truck and an orderly takes care of them for him. All I have to carry is a steel helmet that I wear all the time when with the troops, a cartridge belt and a heavy pair of suspenders that fasten into the belt. They have rings on them to fasten other things on, a musette bag that is on my back and fastened into the suspenders. In the bag I have a raincoat, two pairs of wool socks, four days rations, a pair of underwear and toilet articles. Fastened into my belt is a trench knife, a compass, a first aid packet, two canteens, a drum of 45 Cal. ammo (50 round drum) and four box type magazines of thirty rounds each. On my right shoulder I carry a Thompson sub-machine gun. On my left shoulder I carry a pair of field glasses and dispatch case. In that I have maps, aerial photos, and map reading and drawing instruments, also a message book and a few other small items. Along with this is a service gas mask and a dust respirator. I will also carry a flashlight, but no one has figured just how I am to carry it.

As supply officer, I can say that I have the best equipped company in the regiment. I am very proud of that because it was a big job. I have personally inspected each weapon, each article of clothing and every piece of equipment in the company. It is all in good shape and when we go into combat, I will have the satisfaction of knowing that I did a good job of equipping the company. You probably won't hear from me for awhile, but don't worry, I shall be all right.

Our ships are loaded and we are all set to go. It is a Hell of a lot of work and takes planning to transport an army. Here's hoping that I can eat Christmas dinner at home— Christmas of '43.

> With love to all,
> Howard

Granddaddy returned from his annual summer bus trip to visit his other daughter, my Aunt Zell, and her family in St. Petersburg. For a while he was full of stories about streetcars and pelicans and promised to take me with him someday. But for the time being, South Florida remained as undefined and foreign to me as that place they all now called Overseas. For what was left of the summer, Granddaddy became increasingly uneasy, and I became his constant companion.

⁓✻⁓

The old Ford bounced and kicked up dust as it lumbered down the dirt road bordered on each side by a green corn patch.

"Some fine roastn'ears out there," Granddaddy commented. I saw the barn in the distance and the cheesecloth shade a little ways beyond.

As we came to the clearing where the mule had stopped with the barge it was dragging, several young farmhands began unloading the pads of tobacco and placing them on the big table in the center of the barn. Young colored girls waiting on tables scurried to get the fresh-primed leaves before the stringers gave out of leaves and started hollering.

"Bring me some 'balco," the fat black woman yelled as her pile of leaves dwindled from her stringing table. She leaned over the table with a stance that allowed her upper body to thrust in four-quarter time, not missing a beat as she plunged the four-inch steel needle into the tobacco stem. Her apron was stained green at the waist where the leaves dragged against her.

"Watch her," Granddaddy said, "she's the top stringer—sometimes stringing five hundred and twenty-five sticks a day. That's a right smart—a stick will hold thirty, maybe forty leaves."

I got out of the way of two rackers carrying the sticks of strung tobacco leaves in each hand. They walked toward the colored man in overalls and stained felt hat who punched the sticks up to the hanger standing straddle-legged on rafters up in the barn. He hung the sticks of leaves high in the lofty barn to dry.

"Watch your step, hon," Granddaddy warned as we walked to the back of the barn where there were several pits of charcoal fires smoking, curing the tobacco.

We walked back through the barn toward the car, Granddaddy promising me a soda water at the corner store and maybe a trip uptown.

He stopped at an almost empty barge and lifted the croker sack covering what was left of the load of green leaves and examined them as he always did at each neighbor's farm we visited. We called them neighbors even though their farms were miles apart and out in the country. A retired tobacco farmer himself, Granddaddy was welcome everywhere and expected to show up on any given day. When his friends urged him, he would sometimes fill up the car at the farms' gasoline pumps: something about the Government providing unlimited gas for the farmers. The land was the thing and watching everybody's crops just like your own was a community pastime. Not very often did I hear him pronounce a crop as "no count." He saved that term for any of the workers—white barn boss on down—when they were responsible for a torn leaf, or a man who would let his yard go to seed, or a woman who would serve her family light bread.

అఙ

Miss Lulah followed me to the back of the dark dime store while Granddaddy waited up front by the cash register. She pulled the string of the single light bulb, on then off, as we moved from section to section—past the Morline Pomade and round, big red porous sponges, the Tangee lipstick, and henna rinses until we came to the paper dolls. As my eyes adjusted, I thumbed through the books until I found the one just like the display in the window of Maxine, Laverne, and Patty, the Andrews Sisters, standing in thick cardboard.

Click, click, went the sound of Miss Lulah's high heels on the dark wood floors—an almost echo of the on and off light bulbs. As she ushered me to the front, I glanced at the lipstick again thinking of the tube of slightly orange-tinted Naturale I would be allowed to carry around when I became thirteen and grown up.

2

A Time to
Pluck Up

Soon there would be a cat killing.

I never saw how they did it, but Mama's brother Winston was a good shot, and sometimes before they hustled Ruthie and me into the front of the house, I saw his black truck near the dairy. Everybody said Winston could kill just about anything with a slingshot.

There are too many of them again. Barn cats, wild cats, that's what we call them. I count them from my bedroom window. There are twenty-seven now—creeping and churning around the feed room—spitting and hissing and flicking their paws at each other. It seems the longer they stay around, the bigger their heads are. They already have oversized heads—heads covered with that awful fur that grows close together—coarse and stiff like a shoe brush.

Sally says her cat's fur is soft and silky, and she tries to make me touch it, but I never do.

Once one of them hid in the house, and when I looked for my other bedroom shoe under the bed, there was a figure there sliding back, blinking its green and yellow Lucifer eyes. I was the wild thing then, screaming and yelling and jumping on top of the bed. When it limped and slithered away, I saw it stop and lick a wide gaping sore on its side.

"Don't yaw'll git close to that cat," Josie had warned as she shooed it toward the back door Mama held open.

It took Mama and a lot of Lysol to convince me to sleep in that bed again where disease and infection itself had been crouching and festering underneath. I change into my work clothes as I do every afternoon after school. Even though the cats are at the other end of the dairy, I am afraid the whole pack will run for me before I can reach the door of the bottle-washing room. Running all the way from the back door of the house, I squeeze inside the screened front porch of the dairy, bolt the little latch, and count those huge heads again. I am safe.

I jump on top of two overturned wooden milk crates and begin helping with the bottle washing. Daddy is sudsing the glass bottles—sticking the entire bottle on a spinning wire brush. Ruthie is rinsing. The bottles are soaking in the chlorine vat waiting for me to stand them up to dry in the wire crates ready for tomorrow's milking.

"If a chicken and a half laid an egg and a half in a day and a half . . . ," Daddy asked Ruthie.

They had already begun with the math problems. Even though Ruthie was only in the second grade, she shared a love of these mental exercises like the rest of the family.

My mind wandered, picturing Uncle Howard's letter written to Aunt Mamie a while back. The grown-ups had passed it around the night before as we all sat around the kitchen table. I had glimpsed two pages of problems— pages covered with x's, y's, inches, feet, and yards.

September 4, 1942

Dear Mamie,

I am very glad that you are considerate enough to send me the math problems. I don't know if you are making fun of me or not so I will work them anyway. When I asked you for some problems, I thought maybe you could find some more difficult. Something dealing with a much higher form of math. I still boast that there is no problem that I cannot work. I am judging the future on the past and I have worked them all up to now.

I have one of the very latest books on ballistics, but will not use it in the solution of the problems you sent me. As you know, ballistics is not true math and therefore, is not very interesting. Some time when you see Dr. Ferrell, ask him for a problem, I promise to work it.

Someday I will have to take back some of my big statements, but that will be a happy day for me because I am never so happy as when I am thinking. By the time you get this you will have received my letter asking for the calculus books. I hope you may realize their value to me. They will take my mind from war and in that way alone I can find rest.

When you are talking to Dr. Ferrell, you may tell him that through the use of hyperbolic function and the letter "e" I believe that I have found a concrete value for "i." When I am sure that this value is right, I will tell you more about it.

I am getting along very nicely and I have the best company of them all and will have. The men love me and are afraid of me and that is the way it should be. My ambition is fulfilled. I am a good officer and it stops at that. When this is over I shall try and be a good husband. Maybe to make up for the fact that I was not a very good brother. Love sister-in-law's children for me.

Love to all,
Your brother,
Howard

P.S. I have enclosed all the paperwork for the problems so you will see how I got the answers. It was four and one-third inches that the bullet would drop in 100 yards while traveling at the rate of 2,000 feet per second. (My God, can't you write about something besides bombs and bullets?) Please send the books.

Daddy's whistling brings me back. My hands feel cold and are all shriveled and white, just like I have removed two giant, glovelike Band-Aids. Ruthie and I take off our wet rubber aprons and boots while Daddy hoses the concrete floor. We were finishing up for the day, but it would all begin again when we would be on the milk truck at 5:00 in the morning delivering the milk. Daddy had converted a pickup truck by welding a metal top with four metal poles over the back like a canopy. Ruthie and I would ride on opposite ends of the back running board, gripping the poles real tight when we came to the dirt roads. We had to watch out for mud puddles and keep our feet tucked in enough to escape the snapping, yapping dogs.

But once Ruthie didn't escape the Watsons' dog. We always switched sides on the running board so it would be fair—fair because we would both have to contend with the Watsons' dog at one time or another.

One particular day it had been raining, and humidity had turned the walk from the Watsons' porch sweaty and slick. Ruthie knew to walk slowly to where "Doll" was usually stretched out pretending to be asleep. She realized she must walk slowly and quietly, carrying the two full bottles of milk, and swap them ever so carefully for the empty ones. You couldn't walk fast or run until you were almost a couple of yards away from the milk truck, but it was hard to be that confident. If Doll was nowhere to be seen, we both knew he was lurking somewhere. And he was lurking that day. Around the house he came, lickety-split.

"Walk fast, but don't run, Ruthie," I hollered. She stood it as long as she could, holding her breath, and glancing from side to side, but then she started to run clutching the empty glass bottles close to her. Doll followed with his hoarse bark and clumsy feet. Mrs. Watson appeared on the porch and called the dog back.

I jumped down to meet Ruthie to take the bottles and pull her back on the running board, but she slid and fell near the curb, dropping the bottles—her knee landing on a jagged piece of glass.

When she came from Doctor Ferrell's examining room with Daddy to the waiting room where I was, it was not the black threads sticking out from the angry, seeping red streak running down her leg below the knee, but her face I would always remember.

Her eyes were red from crying, and her face was smeared with the residue of tears wiped and wiped again. There was something now that she held in her eyes, not letting on that she owned. But it was plain enough for me to catch—not like a glance, eyes turned away or lowered—more like something erased and replaced in the seven-year-old face. It was that first encounter with circumstance. Now it was plain that circumstance might not give you a chance to escape a big red scar—or something worse.

Lots of times after that I would get circumstance mixed up with guilt. I would see Ruthie's scar, shiny with Vaseline, and know it could have been me on the Watsons' side of the running board.

Daddy kept on whistling "Country Gardens," the new piece I had been practicing all week. He put up the hose and turned out the lights. We all walked together toward the kitchen door and I headed for the organ.

It had been six months since I had started taking music lessons. I learned to play on the Beckwith three-reed pump organ Daddy bought from the disbanded Gretna Methodist Church for $5.00. After Daddy took the organ apart, he and Mama sanded and refinished each piece of wood. I can see them now sitting in front of the fireplace rubbing and caressing those long pieces of carved oak. After the organ was put back together, tuned, and adjusted, we put it in the living room with the only other furniture—a platform rocker, covered in a dingy beige material with rosy flowers, next to the console radio.

I reached under the glass prisms for the knob to turn on the globe lamps balanced on each side of the organ's "arms." Those little spheres of glass would always brush against the lamp base making soft, tinkling sounds like the dining room chandelier when there was a stiff summer breeze. I tipped back the music rack and pulled out my music. The seat Mama had covered in burgundy faille slanted toward the organ making it a little easier for me to play. I almost stood while leaning back on the seat to reach the wide pedals pressing one and then the other, just like riding my blue and white Schwinn.

I played all my favorite pieces—"Swans on the Lake," "Dublin Town," and "To a Skyscraper." Stretching my hands to sustain the notes and playing slowly, I held each key down tight to make the chords sound rich and full. After playing a simplified version of "Safely Through Another Week," I stopped when Mama called me to set the table.

ॐ

Cooler mornings and evenings brought with them the sweet, juicy taste of sugarcane. Dog days finally gave in to

cane-grinding weather. These were the Saturday afternoons when Granddaddy would take Ruthie and me to a
farm where cane syrup was being made.

Harnessed to the mill that squeezes the cane, the dusty
mule plods around and around in circles. I didn't know if
the mule was so slow because he was tired or because he
was dizzy. The green, yellow, and purple reedlike stalks of
cane are fed into a grinder and crushed between two
turning drums. A tub is there to catch the dripping brown
juice. The cane comes out flat and moist, and the horse-
drawn wagon carries it away to make more huge mounds
for us to tumble on.

We watch as the men skim the foam from the boiling
cane juice until it turns into that precious goo of thick,
amber gold. Granddaddy would alternate between story-
telling and whittling to peeling the cane and cutting it at
the joint—just the right size for us to chew. When we
weren't on the top of the wet cane leavings we were
chewing the cane, spitting out the pulp, and letting the
juice trickle down our throats and down the front of our
shirts.

On the way home, Ruthie and I lie exhausted in a sticky
lump in the back of the old Ford. The soft clinking of
Granddaddy's full syrup bottles next to him lull us to
sleep. I dream of tumbling down huge stacks of flattened
cane stalks with my friends at the Hardy's annual pilau
supper.

That wonderful, wood-smoke smell gushes from about
half a dozen black washpots balanced on bricks over a slow

fire. The men are using boat paddles to stir the chunks of deboned and skinned chicken cooking up thick with the broth-flavored rice seasoned with plenty of black pepper. Sally is at the top of the shredded cane pile. "Come on, Sari, I've already been down seven times."

I climb up the high grassy hill to the big tree around which the heavy wire is attached and stand in line. When it is my turn, I grasp the handle attached to the pulley, which begins to carry me down, down, down to the slippery mesh of cane at the other end of the side yard where the grown-ups are already fixing their plates of pilau, cole-slaw, homemade pickles, saltines, and canned pears.

We play on—climbing, then sliding, our spit blowing past us as we hold the pulley, rushing head on into the cool night air. After we grow tired and hungry, we stand turning our eyes away from the smoke to be served heaping helpings from those black washpots—the same washpots used to wash clothes, make soap, and boil water used to scald slaughtered hogs, loosening their hair to be scraped away.

I had seen hogs split from "stem to stern"—entrails removed and intestines used for sausage casings, shoulders and backbones salted and cooled on the padded pine-branched floor of a smokehouse, a low hickory fire smoking the salted and sugared hams hung from smokehouse rafters with bear grass—grass Granddaddy said was tougher than any string. I remember seeing a low rectangular table covered with a sheet of galvanized metal held in place on the sides by roofing nails. This is where hogs were placed to scrape the hide. The table could be easily hosed down and cleaned afterwards and in my mind was always "the hog-killing table." I had seen all this activity over and over again with Granddaddy in the backyard of kinfolks and neighbors in yards swept so clean that some of the tree roots would be showing like giant gnarled fingers coming out of the ground. These rural backyards were unlike ours in town whose backyards contained a vegetable garden, fig and other fruit trees, a small chicken house, and a maze of azalea and camellia bushes. Our backyard went a step further and included a pecan orchard inside the fenced cow pasture next to the dairy. This cow pasture was covered with pecan trees underneath which the grass and crunchy brown leaves hid the precious nuts just like Easter eggs.

"Sari, you and Ruthie, it's time you made money to buy Christmas presents. I'll pay you the same as the Negras—one-half of everything you put in the big croker sack. Weigh the pecans before you put them in the sack and keep up with it. You'll get paid when we sell the crop," said Daddy.

We line up on our knees with the little colored children who live in the quarters behind the house and search among the manure—fresh and dried—for our Christmas money.

"Dink, those trees are full at the top, see if two of those darkies can climb up there and knock the pecans off with th' fishing poles," Granddaddy said. Ruthie and I were sure to be around after they finished, for the pecans knocked from the tree limbs were just like manna from heaven. Every afternoon we were out in the pasture combing our way and inching through the grass filling our lard cans and emptying them. Ruthie kept up with how much money we were making. We had almost half the money we needed to buy everybody a Christmas present by the time Thanksgiving, my favorite of all holidays, rolled around.

Today is November 20, the opening day of hunting season. It is also the beginning of a series of breakfasts held in Mama's kitchen for the hunters. They are here before dawn enjoying sausage, grits, eggs, and biscuits with fig preserves. I pour hot coffee and hear them talk of how careful they must be with the shells this year. They talk of their favorite hunting places—Oakey Bend, Hickory Hill, Blue Hammock, and the One-Eye Stand. At one such breakfast, I had overheard the story behind this One-Eye business. It had to do with Granddaddy unintentionally killing a one-eyed gobbler. The talk was that Granddaddy had been so embarrassed that he cut off the turkey's head before the rest of the hunters came back to the car. His brother, Uncle Elbert, found the head in a clump of palmettos. From then on they teased Granddaddy and kept at it, soon giving an immortal name to the spot where he gave in to his momentary slide into deception.

The house has been smelling of 3 in 1 oil now for several days. Daddy and Granddaddy would dismantle and rub their shotguns, drop a small weight wrapped in a piece of flannel cloth tied with a string down the gun barrels and continue to grease their boots with neat's-foot oil. They have several days to bag quail, deer, and turkey for our Thanksgiving feast.

The Pilgrims had nothing on us. We always celebrate this holiday with a family reunion in the woods near the bank of the Ochlockonee River where there had once been a brickyard. So not only do we associate Thanksgiving with going to the river, we also call it "going to the brickyard." Granddaddy and Uncle Elbert would always go down to the place and clear a spot a few days before Thanksgiving and build a long table with side seats. They built another table with sand on top to use for some cooking even though most of the cooking was done at home beforehand. We had been chopping celery and onions for several days, and the smell of Mama's dried apple cake had finally pierced the aroma of the gun oil.

Thanksgiving day dawned clear and cool as if the weather had saved up all its best for our day. I felt light and full of energy.

"Over the river and through the woods . . . ," we sang as the car turned into the dirt river road.

Mama held the turkey roaster that had been in our family thirty-five years. It was charred and chipped and had holes in the bottom covered in several places with "mendits," little round metal plugs. Ruthie and I steadied the long rectangular pan of cornbread dressing in our laps, and Granddaddy held the pot of peas. He kept an eye on the pumpkin pie wedged on the floor between his shoes.

As soon as we had hugged everybody and unpacked the food, Ruthie and I began gathering branches of red and yellow autumn leaves, holly, and yaupon berries. We piled them in the center of the long table, arranging fruit and gourds around them. The men and boys started appearing from out of the woods dressed in their hunting clothes. The last cars had arrived, and once again Uncle Elbert delivered the prayer blessing.

"Although our country is at war and our boys are away from home, we still have so many, many blessings for which to be thankful." As was the custom, he spoke at length of the state of our country and of our family, mentioning each one who had crossed the Great Divide. I stood on one foot and then the other.

"We pray for the early ending of hostilities, the re-union of our families, and a lasting peace." "Amen." "Amen." "Amen." It resounded throughout the camp. "When are you gonna' fix your plate and sit down?" Mama asked Aunt Mamie who still stood cutting up turkey. A group of cousins had eaten in a hurry and were slipping away to wander in the woods or wade to the sandbar when no one was looking.

Aunt Mamie circulated among everyone and asked, "Have you signed The Book yet?" She watched every signature overseeing that it was signed in the proper place. Totally in charge, she flipped the pages and found the right spot for each of us. First Generation, Second Generation, Third Generation. We knew who we were.

After we had finished eating, the men sat around the

campfire on bean hampers and talked of their boys who were waiting for their orders—Dan in California, Bill in Jacksonville. It had been several weeks or more since we had heard from Uncle Howard. "We've been making do with his old letters—the ones he wrote before he left the states," I heard Mama say as she tasted somebody's green tomato pickles.

September 22, 1942

Dear Dad,

Today I received your card and the letter from Sari. They made me feel a little ashamed of myself for not writing to you more often. Because I don't write more often than I do, don't feel bad about it. I just damn sure don't have time to write. To begin with, you may continue to write to the same address, that will get to me no matter where I am. For instance, as I write I am in the woods and some little ways from Ft. Bragg.

We have our orders now and know where we are going to attack. We have maps of the place and have studied them until they are very familiar. We are about ready to shove off.

A few days ago I took a physical exam, and was declared fit for overseas duty. I feel like a young colt in a big pasture. If I can only do a good job and make these men a good officer. All training of officers and men has stopped. We are now devoting all our time to last minute preparation.

I am glad to be going as I am tired of getting ready. I sent some papers home about a week ago. Did they arrive? Please put them away where they will be safe. Please let me know if you have them or not. I am going to give up writing. I have been disturbed three times.

> With Love to All,
> Howard

To My Sister-In-Law in Care of Miss Emma at the Post Office
Hello, Miss Emma.

> October 4, 1942

Dear Sister-In-Law:

I hope that when you open this letter you get ashes all over yourself. It serves you right for the way you used to hide my cigars. What have you got in the ice box?

Lib, you know the other day I left to go on an all day mission and took two cans of chow with me, that is two cans per man. It was dark when we got there and what do you think it was—carrots, every can of it. I ate it but I did not have to like it. I got myself all humerated with smoke.

What are you having for supper? Will you fix me some noodles sometime and not ration them out to me? As long as I can get letters from you at home I do not mind my work here. At least I know what I am fighting for.

I sure do miss you, sister-in-law, but somehow I know that I will come back. It will take a silver bullet to get me. I sure wish I was there to go uptown for you. Haul off and write me a long letter. Gather up the girls and hug them for me.

> Your favorite brother-in-law,
> Howard

October 11, 1942

Dear Dink,

I sent Eileen home (to Miami) the first of this week. She didn't like it very much, but knew that it was best and has been very good about it.

About my insurance and other things you asked about, I have taken care of them. I had an allotment of $100.00 per month made to Eileen that is good as long as I am in the army and for six months after I am dead in case I become a casualty while in the service. I have made my will and power of attorney. The insurance I am not through with yet. I am getting $10,000 but it is not made out yet. The allotment to the bank has been taken care of. (All three siblings, Dink, Mamie, and Zell were to receive $1,000 each with the remainder of $7,000 going to Eileen.)

My only worry is about Eileen, she is very lonely. It must be hard for her as she has plenty of time to worry. It hurts me to be in a position where I can't do things for my wife. It seems very unfair to her. All I ask is to be able to come home when the whole mess is over.

I think I have been pretty good about writing to her. I write her at least every other day. She writes me every day, sometimes twice a day. Somehow I feel kind of settled.

I am going to give you my advice about you getting in the army. It is a hard life to lead and is getting worse. You will get use to it, but your wife won't. I would like to see you in the army, but would feel sorry for Lib. The training that you receive won't cure her loneliness. So my final word is that if you see fit to join the army, be ready to give up your people almost completely.

I am sitting here wondering if all of this is worthwhile. I am no longer a man but a machine—a machine that is a little homesick. Maybe I had too good a home. This life here is alright if about once a week you could get away and rest a little. Every time I get a chance to write, I have to use that time for something else. You may think that I could stay up a little later at night so that I could write. I am aching for sleep.

With ever increasing anxiety,
Howard

We stood for group pictures, then for individual family ones. The hair brushing and posing over, we ran to take off our shoes and socks, testing our toes in the shallow, icy river and then sinking them into the wet, white sand of the riverbank. We chased each other in and out of the willows that made a kind of forest near the river's edge. We were Robin Hood, Maid Marian, and Friar Tuck mysteriously appearing from behind a tree. All damp and giggly we played all afternoon with close and distant cousins—all of us surrounded by the musky, distinct, indescribable smell of the river.

3

A Time to Weep

Dear Dad,

This is going to be short. Have been at sea since the 15th of last month. We are now a few miles off the coast of Africa. When you read this you will have heard the president's approximation and will know what the score is. I can see that I am in for a long campaign and will be away for some time. It is going to be a great show at a great cost, we have a splendid cast and a large theater. I am in the best of health and expect to remain that way. You will not hear from me for some time, but do not worry. If you wonder where I am just read where the spherepoint of the second front is and I will be right around there.

It is now the 6th and we are about 200 miles off the coast. Tomorrow night we land. It is thought that we will meet heavy resistance. We know that we are outnumbered but all in all things are in our favor—give my love to all,

Howard

P.S. Please do not worry. I will be home for Christmas dinner 1943. All is set—we can't lose.

P.S. I go over in 2 hrs. Am leaving this with the mess Sgt.

I balanced the long cardboard roll that had held Christmas wrapping paper over my lips. I steadied the roll with one hand as I dropped the small, blue Christmas ball down the tube. I didn't usually do anything but listen and think about what Granddaddy was reading or telling or reciting, but this time he was reading that poem in McGuffy's Readers, "Which?" I guess I was looking for any kind of distraction. It was the story of a poor family who consider giving away one of their children in return for a house and land. "The oldest, the baby, the wayward son?" Granddaddy read on . . . and I kept wondering just how poor we were with the rationing and all. Just the other night, Granddaddy and I had gone to the school auditorium where they were giving everybody stamp books, even babies. We never had birthday cakes anymore unless Mama swapped butter, eggs, or milk with someone willing to give up a few cups of sugar.

The first six times the Christmas ball landed against my lips, but the seventh time, my lips must have parted, so the ball landed hard on my tooth which caused the ball to shatter into thin pieces. I began spitting out pieces of the blue ornament and couldn't explain to anybody or myself how or why I had wound up with a mouth full of blood.

After I got all cleaned up, I was thankful for the chance to stand behind Granddaddy's chair and try to follow the difficult words of a new poem he was reading us tonight:

> Wee, sleekit, cowrin, tim'rous beastie,
> O, what a panic's in thy breastie!
> Thou need na start awa sae hasty,
>   Wi' bickering brattle!
> I wad be laith to rin an' chase thee,
>   Wi' murd'ring pattle!

It had to do with a mouse who had been jostled out of her nest with a plow.

Granddaddy's voice flowed with the Scottish brogue and did not hesitate over the different words or the foreign way he was speaking. I, like him, was trying to lose myself in the spelling and pronunciation so I wouldn't relive the telegram of several days ago.

DECEMBER 19, 1942

MR. BRADFORD:

THE SECRETARY OF WAR DESIRES ME TO EXPRESS HIS DEEP REGRET THAT YOUR BROTHER, SECOND LIETENANT WILLIAM HOWARD BRADFORD WAS KILLED IN ACTION IN DEFENSE OF HIS COUNTRY IN NORTH AFRICA NOVEMBER 8. LETTER FOLLOWS.

ULIO THE ADJUTANT GENERAL

My dear Mr. Bradford:

It is with deep regret that I learned of the death of your brother in North Africa.

I realize that there is little that can be said to alleviate your grief, but I hope that you will derive some consolation in the knowledge that Howard Bradford served with honor in the United States Army and died in the best traditions of the service. To men like your brother who have died that the American way of life can continue, the nation owes an everlasting debt of gratitude.

Again, my deepest sympathy to you and to other members of the family.

Faithfully yours,
George C. Marshall
Chief of Staff

We went through the motions of Christmas, but it felt like everything had been shut down. Things were too loud and too bright, but Mama insisted we all keep busy and keep involved in the spiritual meaning of Christmas. As usual, we gathered smilax, full of berries this year, from the back fence for the front door swag and mantelpieces. White cotton batting covered the mantel top and hid the string of all yellow lights we used to light the insides of our cardboard houses we had made the year before. We had painted them and covered the rooftops with more cotton batting and silver glitter. Our homemade papier-mâché reindeer stood around the houses we had once called friendly.

"And lo the Angel of the Lord appeared," read Miss Cahill. The smallest first grader, dressed in wings and halo, came down from Mr. Hardy's pulley across the stage of the high school auditorium landing at the feet of the shepherd and saying: "Fear not, for unto you a child is born."

After the fifth and sixth graders sang "It Came Upon Midnight Clear," the scene changed to my scene—the manger scene where I sat reverently, my hair covered in Mama's blue tablecloth. In my arms I cradled last year's doll.

Miss Cahill had said that there would never be anyone who could play Jesus Christ in a play or at the picture show. This was because there was no perfect person. The way she looked at me sometimes during rehearsals, I wondered if she felt the same way about Mary.

I got my very own Bible, my name in gold on the front, from Granddaddy with the inscription written in his own unique hand. It was more than penmanship—almost calligraphy, the flourishes he used. I always thought of him when Miss Cahill told us in Bible Class at school how the monks sit all day and copy the Bible making those beautiful manuscripts. I had watched him often at his desk carefully refilling his fountain pen and writing his letters to Uncle Howard. Once I peeked and read over his shoulder:

Remember there was a fourth in the fire with the Hebrew children and one who walked on the wind-tossed waters of

Galilee and said, "Peace be still." We will continue to pray for you and God will spare you and bring you back. Take Him for your guide and he will in no way forsake you. He says the world cannot pluck you from his hand. Keep your religion. He can and will keep you from all harm. Be of strong faith always.

Daddy worked hard at his typewriter, getting a letter off to the war department:

Richland, Florida
December 25, 1942

Regimental Commander
Co. "B" 60th Infantry
Ft. Bragg, N.C.

Dear Sir:

I received a telegram from the War Department in Washington on the 19th of this month saying that my brother, Second Lieutenant William Howard Bradford, 34023684, was killed in action in Africa on November 8th.

I was told by a soldier that if I would write to you I could get more information as to my brother's death. I would like to know how he was killed, and if he was killed instantly, and what his last words were. Surely some of his comrades would know this.

I am enclosing a picture of some graves in North Africa, wondering if one could be my brother's. If so, I would like to have it pointed out and returned to me.

If this letter does get to the company that my brother was in, I would like to hear from some of the boys that knew him.

Thanking all who may write me some information, and
wishing for the safe return of all back home some day,
Yours in the cause of freedom,
C. B. Bradford, Jr.

I found out about a lot of things this Christmas—Santa
Claus among others, but I never told anybody. Way back
during late summer, when we were all in the cedar closet
hiding from lightning, I saw the foot of a brand new doll
sticking out from a stack of quilts. And I recognized the
flannel material of our new nightgowns as the bolt of cloth
I had seen on one of the shelves. Besides feeling unworthy
of being Mary, I also came to question obligation and a
thing called Christian duty.

The preacher thought it was the thing to do—borrow a
flatbed truck and pump organ and send our Sunday School
class on a charity mission to deliver old and new toys to the
needy. I pumped the organ and played Christmas hymns
while our truck followed the faded tracks of the over-
grown road. The grass on either side was up over the
running board, and the grass in the middle slowed us
down as we made our way.

The light in the distance was dim as we headed into a
little clearing that made me think of Hansel and Gretel.
The first things I saw were pine boughs twisted around a
coat hanger hanging on the front door for a wreath. Paper
chains of red and green construction paper framed the
windows. A kerosene lamp shone from the one where a
little girl's face was pressed like a moth to the pane.

The mother came out and accepted the sacks from Brother Kittle, and I was thankful I had to look at the notes as the rest sang, "God Rest Ye Merry Gentlemen." It seemed like we had been trespassing as we left singing "We wish you a Merry Christmas." We were "doing good" where good enough was being done, and in performing our duty had brought the curtain down on a mother's magic.

In another faraway country, another brand of true Christmas miracle was coming about:

DECEMBER 29, 1942

MR. BRADFORD

REFERENCE MY TELEGRAM DECEMBER 19 REPORTING YOUR BROTHER
SECOND LIEUT WILLIAM H BRADFORD INFANTRY KILLED IN ACTION
REPORT NOW RECEIVED FROM AFRICAN AREA STATES YOUR BROTHER
IS SLIGHTLY WOUNDED AS RESULT ENEMY CAPON NOVEMBER 19
PERIOD REPORTS WILL BE FORWARDED WHEN RECEIVED

ULIO THE ADJT GENERAL

January 1, 1943
Miami, Florida

Dear Dad,

I hardly know what to say. It's all been such a shock but the last one such a wonderful shock that I'm still in more or less of a fog. We can certainly thank God for being so wonderful to us.

A letter arrived from Howard New Year's Eve Day postmarked November 29th. In my haste to get it out of the mailbox I fell and dislocated my shoulder and am writing this with my arm in a sling. Consequently, please forgive the illegibility of this. Shall copy parts of it.

My dear wife,

To keep from boring the censors, this will be short. We had a nice reception here, one that I shall not forget right away. During the activities I got something that looks like a rifle ball through my left thigh. For the past week or so, I have been taking it easy in the hospital. I will be here for another week or so and then return to duty.

The food here is probably the best in Africa. We eat three hot meals each day. Among the casualty list the only one you would know is Sgt. Wicker. He was killed the first thing. That is going to be a hard blow to his wife. Things are quite peaceful here now. (Please continue to write to my old address.)

I am beginning to realize how much I miss you. I miss you plenty. Maybe it won't be so long before I shall be with you all the time. This thing is coming to an end soon. Maybe in a year from now I will be recognized as an expert coon hunter. Please take good care of yourself and don't worry about me. I am alright and shall be alright.

P.S. Do you think you could cook a coon?
P.P.S. Don't worry about the coon, I couldn't catch one anyway.

That's it, Mr. Charlie. Somehow, I feel that Howard will not be sent into combat again. Officers here say that they're usually not, once they have been wounded. Let's pray that it's so.

Also, the purpose of these replacement centers is to send men overseas to relieve those who are there so that they may come home. Perhaps we'll see him soon. Isn't it wonderful though? Before Howard left he told me one time that he knew he would come back, but he had a feeling something would happen to his left leg and sure enough that's what happened.

If I can get the time off, I hope I can come up to see you for a day or two. I'm going to see about a leave of absence this week.

Thank you for advancing me the money. I'm very thankful I haven't got to use it.

I still haven't received my allotment but that doesn't seem important anymore.

> Much love to you, Mr. Charlie
> Eileen

Uncle Howard had survived—turning the grief and uncertainty of that Christmas season into a finish not unlike that of the serials at the Saturday afternoon picture show. Because I knew the hero had jumped from the stagecoach just before the explosion, I continued to believe in hope and trust. Good men last.

> Northwest Africa
> Nov. 26, 1942

Dear Dink,

From where I am sitting I can see the ocean. I am in a

hospital that is right on the beach. When the sun is setting I look out to the west and somehow it has a meaning that looking to the west never had before.

The people here were very glad to have us for they gave us quite a reception. In the course of events, I got a rifle ball right through the center of my left thigh. I am getting along fine and will return to duty in about a week. All is under control now.

The hills here are high and are in long ridges. The mountains are snow-capped and there are some large and beautiful cities here. This is a very old country with a lot of interesting things to see. I very likely will see plenty of it before I get out of here. The money is cheap as Hell but you can't buy anything because there is nothing to buy. The country seems to have been cleaned out. How the Arabs live I do not know. This is a wonderful place to sit at home and read about. I have seen a great show and from the way things look, I shall see more. (Along about hog-killing time don't you know I am going to be homesick?) Eat a piece of sausage for me and I hope it is good and hot.

This is all great fun but somehow I shall be glad when it is over.

It will be over soon now. For a lot of us, it is all over.

The mail service is not the best in the world and I have no idea when you will get this. By that time I will be in action again. I am with some of the finest men in the world and these men like me. That is really what counts. They come to see me everyday and bring me whatever they can get. To be with men like these is a privilege. No power on earth can beat the American soldier.

When I get home, I plan to do some serious resting. That

will amuse Lib. If things get a little hard at home just make the most of it, but don't complain. Be thankful that you are an American. I am only now learning the real meaning of being an American.

My Battalion Commander came to see me a few days ago and while here gave me some very nice remarks. One compliment coming from him makes this whole damn thing worthwhile.

I have not received any mail since I left the states some while back.

There was an accident a few minutes ago. A truck turned over. There are three dead and the nine injured have been brought in.

Most of the men here don't like the idea of stopping. They want to keep on going. So do I for we all have the feeling that by fighting is the only way for us to get home. I think that if I get home again, I shall never leave the country.

There seems to be no tobacco here. All I have had for the last few weeks have been cigarettes.

I would give my good leg to be able to see Sari now. I am going to write a line now that the censors may take out. Please never give anything to the Red Cross. I just got the word that one of my best friends died last night. When an Armistice is signed that does not mean that everything is all over. I am a much wiser man than I was a few years back. Maybe wise is not the right word, but I have seen some things that I did not know before. I have just been interrupted to have a new dressing put on my leg. The doctor says I will be out in a few days. We have been on "C" rations. If you don't know what "C" rations are, you are lucky. I will write again soon. Please give my love to all. Tell Lib that I dreamed about her last night.

When you write, please give me the figures of my bank statement. I won a little over $800.00 on the way over here. I hope that I can get the money out of here and send it home.

Your brother,

Howard

Northwest Africa

November 29, 1942

Dear Dad,

As I write, I am sitting up in bed, looking out of the window at one of the most beautiful days I have ever seen. It is very calm and not a cloud in the sky. It is just cool enough to make one feel good. It is just such a day as I have seen at the Brickyard.

This Thanksgiving I have more to be thankful for than ever before. I am glad to be an American. Today we will have turkey and all the trimmings. This country is as bare as "Mother Hubbard's cupboard" and only an American soldier could have turkey here.

Along with the thankfulness, I feel something else of a different nature. Hate. My heart is getting full of it. I have changed so much that I will not be good company when I get home. A man with hate in his heart is no good.

From the news standpoint things look good. If the people back home keep sending us supplies and more men, we will all be home soon.

The Commanding General pinned a metal on me the other day. It is a very pretty metal, but one that I did not want, a Purple Heart. I am thankful to be able to receive it, but one is enough. I don't want anymore.

You can buy French Champagne here for 80 cents a quart. It may please you to know that I would not be interested. I am waiting until I get home. From a money standpoint, I am doing all right. I am still the best poker player I ever met.

I hope to be released from the hospital tomorrow and go back to duty. There is very little I can say about this place as I have seen very little of it. Maybe in a week or so I will write again and by then I will have seen more of the place to write about.

I am wondering what another Thanksgiving will bring.

Before I left Bragg, I sent some papers home. They were in a large envelope. Did you get them? If so, just put them where they will be safe.

There seems to be no tobacco here. For a cigar, I would give my right arm.

Please give my love to all. If I write seldom, don't worry. It is not always convenient to do so. My address has changed:

Lt. William H. Bradford
Co. "B": 60th C.T.
A.P.O. #9
C/o Postmaster
New York, N.Y.

I hope you are all well. I am in the best health and feel really good. I may be a little weak for the first few days when I get back to my outfit, but I will recover soon.

Howard

January 27, 1943

Dear Dink,

To start with, I ain't dead and am a Hell of a long way

from it. In fact, I have no idea of dying anytime soon. I received the letter you sent to my regional commander. The letter came straight to me as it was addressed to "B" Company. The mail orderly saw the return address on the envelope and brought it to me.

Time I read it, I got permission from my Battalion Commander to go see the head of the Adjutant General's Office. He said that he would get a cable off to make a correction. On November 8th I had a close call, maybe, and was thought by some to be dead but I have never been in as good health before as I am right now. The picture you sent is the right one. The two men guarding the graves are my own men and if I had been dead on November 8th that is where I would have been buried. Those graves were later moved to a larger graveyard. That is what we call temporary burial.

The mistake on the part of the war dept. is a serious one. My name is being dropped from the records and my pay will stop and in a few weeks the war dept. will try to pay off my insurance—a Hell of a mess if you ask me. I should go ahead and die just to keep the books straight. Later I will send you a picture of the permanent graveyard where you can read the names on all the graves. I have a lot of friends there, including my old company commander.

This letter has caused a lot of talk with the Battalion. We all think it is a big laugh but we all realize the seriousness of it back home. I only hope that this letter gets through. I will write one each week or two apart. Maybe one of them will get to you.

I am returning the letter and the picture. You may know how glad I am that none of the graves are marked. I wish you would keep all of this for me as it was a very unusual let-

ter, one like few people, if any receive. I hope that you and
the rest at home are in as good health as I am.

>Love to All,
>
>Your brother,
>
>Howard.

Come, fill the Cup, and in the Fire of Spring
The Winter Garment of Repentance fling:
The Bird of Time has but a little way
To fly—and Lo. The Bird is on the Wing.

Granddaddy recited from the back seat of the car while
Daddy drove. Now on Sunday afternoons we didn't go far
because of the gasoline shortage, but we always took our
one Spring trip to the river.

Sometimes we would cross over the Old Iron Bridge to
check on the river, turn around in Leon County, and drive
back over it. I always dreaded riding over it—a look-
forward-to-dread like riding the Hardy's cable to the
sugarcane mounds.

The bridge groaned and clanked under us as we crept
over the loose, wooden planks. "We're comin' to the river
now, Sari. Tell me how it looks today." With a quick
glance, I was to report whether it was high or low, clear or
muddy. We finally made it and took a sharp right turn to
the dirt road. While looking for animal tracks in the
middle of the road, I thought I caught a whiff of that
strong, wild, and appealing river smell—decaying wood
and bedding fish in the dark, murky water.

I helped Mama carry an armload of white wild plum and redbud to the car trunk. Daddy was breaking off the high limbs of dogwood for Ruthie. Tomorrow the house would be filled with massive bouquets of flowering tree blossoms—a sure sign of spring and a very special birthday.

March 18, 1943

Dear Dink,

For the last six days I have been where I could not receive mail. Today I got 11 letters. Last night was a Hell of a night. I thought that I would never forget it, but when I got my work done and returned to my dug-out and found a letter waiting for me I forgot the whole damn thing for a while.

I will quote the last half of a sentence in your letter of February 16.

"So on Sunday, February 7th, the same day Uncle Elbert died, Mary Howard Bradford was born."

I looked at that until my eyes filled with tears and I could see it no longer. The death of Uncle Elbert did not cause the tears, for I rather expected it and have lost many friends.

My mind went back some nine years ago to the night the first little girl was born and the others each in their turn. It brought me up to date—7 February. It so happened that on that day, I took several lives. So in the years to come, Mary Howard's birthday will remind me of many things—of some things she shall never know about.

Your brother,
Howard

P.S. I have learned that History is much easier to read than it is to make. I see a runner coming towards me and I am expecting the worst—two to one it is.

A few weeks later a package came for Mary Howard. It was a sterling silver napkin ring with the initials M.H.B. from Eileen.

⚜

It was Sunday afternoon and my first recital in front of the parents on Miss Ruby Tidwell's piano in her living room. The gladioli and fern corsage pinned to the shoulder of my brand new lavender dotted-swiss dress tickled my chin as I whispered to Ruthie, "I'm next." I handed her the twisted roll of sheet music. It would make too much noise now to open it and look at it one more time.

When I hit the first chord, I knew. Nothing had prepared me for what a piano could do to my organ rendition of "Long, Long Ago." Into the first measure the keys felt loose and floppy under my fingertips. My hands did not know this touch. With no effort, the sound rushed at the slightest touch and didn't stay. It was like I was trying to catch the keys flying free from the keyboard like a Mickey Mouse cartoon. Faster and faster I played—picking up speed at a roller coaster pace, and there was nothing to do with my feet. There were no wide pedals to push.

After that, I began practicing at the church on the piano in Mrs. Pettaway's Sunday School room. Even though the superintendent had given me permission, I always had a feeling I was doing something wrong in "God's House"—hitting all those wrong notes and not just playing hymns. Besides, going back and forth to the church every day cut into the time I needed for all my chores.

"Girls, get started on the living room while I finish hemming these two evening dresses for the Holman twins," said Mama as she handed me the can of Johnson's Paste Wax. "I need to have these dresses finished. They're picking them up in about an hour," she added as she went back through the double doors. I knew Mama needed to collect the money for her dressmaking to pay Mrs. Scruggs, my music teacher, this afternoon.

"Sari, hold the baby and I'll get your feet ready," said Ruthie. I sat in the rocker holding my little sister while Ruthie wrapped my feet mummy-style in a worn-out pair of Granddaddy's long underwear without the buttons. After I wrapped hers, I began spreading the paste wax as evenly as I could over the hardwood floors of the living room—as empty and expansive as the local City Hall. It was so big and so bare—we pretended we were in a skating rink. Ruthie found a waltz on the radio and we moved to the music—sliding and gliding until the whole floor and our faces were glowing. We practiced our Sonja Henie turns, watching our reflections in the French doors leading to the dining room where Mama sewed. We now had a new ritual to even up all the streaks we might have missed. Mama had covered the bottom of a gun shell box with pink flannel, now slick and gray from the wax buildup. Because our baby sister was too young to sit up, we laid her in the box and strapped her in with one of Daddy's belts we wrapped around the box and buckled over her chubby stomach. She reminded me of a little turtle overturned on its back. A plump, gurgling mass with flailing arms and legs, she smiled and cooed as we pulled her across the floor—her weight just right for buffing the floor to its final shine.

જ

It was hard to tell the exact age of Mrs. Scruggs. By the way she dressed, she could have easily been anywhere from fifty to seventy-five. Every Saturday she came by bus from Old Salem to teach piano lessons. She carried a faded, tapestry bag that had no clasp, just two handles that came together like those of a knitting bag. She clutched the bag as if the sheet music, the Etudes, and the John Thompsons inside were something very private. In the other hand, she always carried her pocketbook and umbrella. She wore, year around, nude cotton stockings and laced black oxfords. Her clear blue eyes matched the softness of her face and the way she wore her gray-brown hair piled loosely on top of her head; she could have easily been kin to us.

This Saturday I noticed that Mrs. Scruggs had pinned a new bouquet of artificial pansies to her dress just below the brooch she always wore at the top button. Her neck and bosom were dusted with just a trace of talcum powder, and she smelled a little of faded lilies. I saw the pansies while she was reaching into her bag to bring out the special piece of music she handed me.

"Sari, I believe you are ready for this now," she said as she gave me the copy of Beethoven's "Fur Elise." I could hardly wait to go to the church to try it out. The arpeggios would be too difficult to connect on the organ. But as I followed her to the porch after my lesson was over and watched her climb into Granddaddy's Ford starting for the bus station, I knew that this would be one of the days Mrs. Scruggs would finally use her umbrella. I had better stay at home.

It was already dark outside, and it was only the middle of the afternoon. I watched from the front porch as the wind rearranged the leaves of the camphor trees. In place of the glossy, dark green of the leaves, the gusts were flipping them over showing a gray-green underside—the wrong side, like the wrong side of some of Mama's Dan River polished cotton.

As soon as Granddaddy came back from town and we had all the cows in the barn, all of us huddled in the hall like we always did when bad weather was coming up. The hall was the safest place. "Never stand in front of a draft, a window, a fireplace," Granddaddy had always warned. So here we were standing in front of nothing. "Open the windows and doors to release the pressure," Daddy explained.

As if Josie hadn't already scared us to death: "Now when it's lightning, keep your feet off the floor, don't touch metal, and don't make a sound." She would repeat this time and time again while herding me, Ruthie, and the baby into the cedar closet. Mama stored our winter clothes and her scraps of material in the closet, which soon came to smell—reeking of cedar and wool, then urine.

The wind whistled and rain came down. The hail sounded like popcorn on the tin roof. I imagined the tall pines outside swaying like oversized, flexible match sticks threatening to strike the heavens. "The tobacco crops will be ruined," Granddaddy predicted. I always had the sensation that I was tied to a roulette wheel like the knife thrower's assistant and the next bolt of lightning wouldn't just graze my shoulder or clear the top of my head, but . . .

After the weather cleared, we rode around in Daddy's truck and looked over the damage. I saw flattened tobacco barns. Cheesecloth was torn and shredded, lying over tobacco crops like exaggerated cobwebs. Sheets of tin had been partially removed from tenant houses as easily as you roll back a sardine can with a key. Trees were uprooted everywhere. The Ulmers' brick house had been almost destroyed except for the one room they had all been in. Mrs. Ulmer was a member of Aunt Mamie's bridge club and I heard her ask Daddy, "Dink, do you suppose you have enough room to store my piano until the house can be rebuilt? Might take several months—a year maybe."

For the next eight months, when I wasn't working in the dairy or going to school, I spent most of my time in the living room. The upright spinet had been placed in front of the living room windows opposite the organ, the radio, and the rocking chair. The room was almost balanced now. I could practice my finger exercises—play Rondo, Allegro, Staccato. I could practice difficult runs with the right hand connecting the arpeggios with the left. The metronome was set higher and higher as the accuracy and pace of my scales increased. I was thrilled to be able to cross one hand over another. If I wasn't playing, I was drifting and dreaming in the rocking chair—seeing myself on the concert stage. The new female Jose Iturbi. During the summer and into the fall, the piano filled my days.

Finally the Ulmers' house was finished and the day came for the piano to be taken away. I played as much as I could early that morning before and after my dairy chores. At school, I dreaded going home—home to the empty space and back to the organ again. Even if I planned not to I knew I would look at the empty space just like I would always turn and look at the cats I didn't want to see—count them when I didn't want to know what happened to the rest of them.

After school I talked longer than usual with Sally and Mary Jean and took my time walking home. I looked in the mailbox for mail Mama had already found. The only reason we got mail on the route, even though we lived in town, was because it was on the way home for Mr. Lester Bevis, the mail carrier. Mr. John continued to watch me from his front porch rocker across the street, his feet propped up on the porch railing. He would have seen Devone and the Jefferson Furniture truck back up close to the side of our porch. When they took it away, they probably wrapped it in those same quilts they had brought it in. As I got closer to the steps, I noticed each periwinkle that drooped over the front walk and the little shoots of border grass that had started to grow in the cracks of the pavement. I walked up the front steps preparing myself for the emptiness.

Instead, I opened the door to the smell of something new. Opposite the organ, the console radio, and the platform rocker was a brand new baby grand piano covering the rectangle of unwaxed floor.

4

A Time
to Heal

They had bought the piano with the money Uncle Elbert had left us and wouldn't you know it—the recital at the school auditorium is just three weeks away. Ruthie and I have the two weeks' measles—the hard, red kind.

I'm sick of listening to Jack Smith and Queen for a Day on the radio. Those women embarrass me instead of making me feel sorry for them. They talk about needing a new winter coat for their crippled mother or a set of dentures for themselves so they can find a job. And all this hanging on the outcome of the applause meter. I can imagine what they must look like all wrapped up in an Old King Cole robe and the winner wearing that bloated Drum Major's hat.

Ruthie and I are in our bedroom with the blinds closed,

lights out, all except for the little green window of the radio. Josie keeps bringing us hot tea so our rashes will keep on "breaking out." I sometimes take quick glances at the "Zampa Overture" I keep by my bed. Maybe I can memorize a few measures at a time without ruining my eyes. Josie says sometimes people go blind or lose their minds if they aren't careful while they have the measles. So Ruthie and I can't do anything but listen to the radio and sculpt the modeling clay animals we form mostly by feel. In the dark we shape the trunks of elephants, necks of giraffes, and the big bodies and legs of rhinoceroses. Granddaddy combines all the correct body parts for us. Pushing toothpicks inside the figures to make them sturdier, he can now line them up on the night table between our beds. He has moved his favorite rocking chair into our bedroom and reads to us and tells us stories to pass the time. Circumstances in the disguise of the measles are stranding us here in this room, and there is no use thinking about being anywhere else. This isolation makes me think of Uncle Howard camping and resting, locked-in, in the country he describes in his last letter.

"Granddaddy, read us about what Uncle Howard says about Africa," I beg. He pulls out the letter from his shirt pocket, the one he doesn't keep his pipe in, and begins.

North Africa
June 1, 1943

Dear Dad,
  "And what is so rare as a day in June

Then if ever come perfect days
'Tis then that Heaven trys earth
To see if she is in tune."
Well, I am afraid that the wild earth is not in tune, but there is not so much discord here in North Africa.

As I look to the west, I see the sky a beautiful golden color, the sun has gone behind the mountain, but there is still another hour of the day left. You see, we are in a valley. There are pines here and reminds me very much of North Carolina.

Funny, I thought, I didn't think there were any trees there at all. I thought it was a desert. I closed my stinging eyes and pictured Uncle Howard in a strange land. I wondered if people saw those places only if they went to war. All I knew about war was what I had seen at the picture show—The Movietone News with that Voice. There was never a person on the screen speaking, but The Voice looming from nowhere, absolutely matter-of-fact, undisputed, the Voice of the Newsreel. Soldiers marched and saluted all in a row, and the artillery fired from under the tents of wide fish net, everything distorted. The jerky movements of soldiers and sounds—out of whack. I kept looking for Uncle Howard in those blurred flashes of black and white.

I couldn't conceive how far it was across water and land to where he was or how long it took letters to travel back and forth and what you couldn't write about and what you could. Of course, Ruthie and I were told hardly anything that was in the letters—just the parts the grown-ups wanted us to know. But it seemed that now what Uncle Howard wrote was always secondhand news coming weeks, even months, later.

It is true that I censor my own mail, but I would not take any privileges.

Well, Dad, I was in the very first fighting and followed through to the very last. When Bizerta fell, we were marching as fast as possible to get there and were only 17K away when we got the news that all was over. You should have seen that column of men I had. We were ragged and tired but willing to fight until it was over. I was marching at the back of my company. Somehow I felt that we would not ever get to Bizerta and when I got the order to halt I knew that I was the happiest man of the lot. We took thousands of prisoners and that is a lot of men to handle. We had our hands full, but now it is all in the past.

At the present time I am in Central Algeria. We are enjoying a much needed rest. The men get just enough exercise to keep fit and the rest of the time just lay in the woods and rest.

Do you remember when I left I said that all I wanted was to be a good officer? I have made good and know that my effort was well spent. The men have every confidence in the world in me. They have proven it many times. We have seen lots of fighting: four major battles and many small engagements. That is more than any unit in our army was in—this or any other war. I hope that we are through. If they keep pushing us up against an enemy, we are bound to all be killed.

June 2

I got interrupted so many times last night until I did not
get to write much before it got dark. It is now 2:00 P.M. and
hot as Hell. You remember how the sun bore down the day
we were packing squash? It is hot here now and I love it. At
last I am warm. There is a lot of glare here and I am having
killing headaches every afternoon. I will be happy when my
glasses come. Yesterday I got six letters from you and two
from Eileen and best of all, one from sister-in-law. Boy I sure
get mad if I don't get mail and I get homesick when I do.
When you use V-mail, please use a pen, it is being photo-
graphed now and is hard to read if in pencil.

Dad, there is little or no game in these woods. I think the
insects eat everything up. There are a few jackals. They howl
at night very much like coyotes. I have learned to speak
very good French, two words, in fact.

"He didn't say what those words were, did he,
Granddaddy?" interrupted Ruthie.

"No," said Granddaddy, "but he goes on to tell about
the French soldiers."

The French are good fighters. For about two weeks I
fought side by side with the French Foreign Legion. They are
a hard crew. Everything but a white man in the bunch. They
handle theirs with the fist system. It is a good system, but very
hard on the fist.

I can tell you where I have been. As you know, I landed
at Mehdia. That is 6 miles south of Port Lyautey. My mission
was to take and hold the airport at Port Lyautey. I fulfilled

that mission. When we left the cork woods at Lyautey, we went by train to Tebbessaa, a native city up in the mountains of Northern Algeria. It was there that we camped in this olive grove. From there we went to Constantine and then to the Kasserine Pass. There we learned many, many things. It was a hard drive from there on. ElGuettar, Maknassy. There is where we caught hell and there is where we contacted the British 8th Army. It was "B" company that made the first contact. From Maknassy we went north through Gafsa to the coast at LaCalle and started another drive. It was called the Battle of the Sedjamine Valley. The day the Battle of the Sedjamine Valley ended, we started the Battle of Bizerta. That was short and sweet, very sweet. For people who would like to see the effects of war, I would recommend a trip to Bizerta. I have seen the sights of Carthage. We did as good a job on Bizerta as the Trojans did at Carthage. The extent of my travels here is from Casablanca to Tunis. The most beautiful is Casablanca. The most unusual is Constantine. They are all very modern. The cities here are much more modern than our own cities back home. Constantine is in the center of the wheat country. The city itself is in the mountains with a gully running through it that is larger than the Grand Canyon. There are taller buildings there than there are in Jacksonville and they are all well made. The town is on five different levels and the streets are connected by tunnels and suspension bridges. To see the city from a distance it looks more like a painting of a City of the Future. One thing in common with these places, they all smell the same—like an Arab.

Mama arrives at the bedroom door with Brother Kittle. "And how are the Bradford girls this evening?" he asked. He had been to see us last week. There was something about his visits that made me uneasy. I should know by now that he came to visit and pray even if you only had a minor cold or a typhoid shot. But I secretly imagined that I had some incurable disease they weren't telling me about. Brother Kittle was even known to hold prayer on the sidewalks. That's right. After conversation with anyone he would pause for a word of prayer. It was a strange-looking thing—Brother Kittle praying and women bowing their heads while standing on the street corner shifting bags of groceries or squirming children.

Just as Granddaddy and I would seat ourselves at one of those octagonal glass-top tables in Sutton's Drug Store, he could time his mission so as to interrupt my sipping on a limeade or a cherry smash. Across the street in front of the Richland State Bank was his favorite stomping ground. Men would stand frozen to the spot holding their open tobacco pouches in one hand, their pipes in the other.

"And make his face to shine upon you. . . ." Mama offered the preacher a piece of pear pie, so Granddaddy began the letter again where he had left off.

I just had to leave again. The Col. came up and wanted to look the company area over. I was glad of it for I knew the area was ship-shape. The thing you and Dink would like about this place is the pretty horses and women. They are both in the pink of condition at this time of year. Honestly, Dad, the little town of Sid Bou Zid would run you crazy. Your neck is too short to see all the sights at once. I went to town one afternoon and came back a nervous wreck so I have not been since.

In case my last letter did not arrive, I asked for a duplicate of the last pair of glasses I got in Tallahassee. Give my best to all.

With love,
Howard

"When do you think he'll be home?" I asked. He hadn't mentioned the war ending in any of his letters. Granddaddy didn't answer but folded up the letter as he slowly eased out of his rocking chair and walked in little shuffles closing the bedroom door behind him.

I wondered how Uncle Howard felt in a foreign land with people he had never known fighting on his side as well as against him. I had lived with the same people that had known me and my family forever. Day in and day out, there was the same cycle of dairy chores, the same house, familiar food, pecans to pick up under the same trees year after year for the same property taxes.

Everybody in Richland had always looked out for the little differences of other people or just plain overlooked them, making allowances. Like watching out for Granddaddy when he was driving.

"Granddaddy, you didn't stop back there and there was a car coming and you had a Stop sign."

"He sees me, Sari," he would say, "He sees me, hon."

And then there was Mary Jean's Daddy and his crooked hand. Every year the town would have a Santa Claus parade. The Merchants' Association would tie up cellophane bags of apples, oranges, nuts, and raisins on stems. The high school band would march, and Santa Claus would arrive on the town fire truck. When we told Santa what we wanted for Christmas, nobody was afraid of the twisted hand holding out the sack of treats. We knew it was Mr. Pearson behind the false face.

It was the predictability, I suppose—the people you could count on to be the same. They, the community and my life all marbled together, sheltered and safe.

After Ruthie switched off the Bell Telephone Hour, I heard Brother Kittle's car backfire down the street.

Hazel Guntry would tell the next day how she had been sitting on her front porch after supper when she saw Hugh Polk's Model A Ford circle the block about four times. Hazel lived across the street from the Polks. Mrs. Mattie Polk and her beautiful, seventeen-year-old daughter, Ellie, lived with her mother, Mrs. Mac, short for Mrs. McCrary. I was allowed to call her that—she was Sally's grandmother.

The Polks' separation was the first of its kind in Richland. I think some of the people living out in the country had these family problems, but until now, it was unheard of in town. Everybody knew Mr. Polk drank a lot, and Mrs. Mac had just run him off. Mama never liked me to visit over there with Sally. When she did give me permission, Sally's cousin Ellie was especially nice to me. She would always take her Shirley Temple doll out of the tissue paper and let me hold it for awhile. Sometimes she would wrap a scarf around her head like a turban, and we would hold mysterious sessions with her Ouija board.

Hazel saw Mr. Polk's car stop in front of the house and Mr. Polk craning his neck to see inside the screened front door. She had thought he was looking to see if Mrs. Mac was home. After sitting in the car for about ten minutes, it seemed to Hazel, Mr. Polk walked up the front steps. Ellie was standing in the living room ironing. The iron cord was plugged into the light socket overhead—the single bulb illuminating her dark hair—her smooth olive skin. "How're you doing, baby?" asked her Daddy. "What 'cha ironing?"

"My dress to wear tomorrow. It's the last day of school and we're doing a special folk dance."

"You'll be the prettiest one there. Where's your Mama?"

"Back in the kitchen. She's finishing the dishes," said Ellie, as she sprinkled the bright red skirt with more water. The iron sizzled as it bonded the starched cotton skirt to the sheet wrapped and pinned around the ironing board. She released the stiff smooth section of cloth from its hold, turning to another and then another wide expanse of skirt as she continued to iron. The entire room had the clean, fresh smell of clothes that had been dipped in liquid Argo starch. It wasn't unusual for her Daddy to visit or to be drunk. She could hear their voices from the back of the house, her mother's tense, her daddy's slurred. The skirt now ironed to perfection, Ellie picked up the damp clump of blouse at the end of the ironing board. She tackled the puffed sleeves first—admiring how expertly her Mama had made the armholes fit. No puckering anywhere. She spread the gathers and ironed the sleeves with the tip of her hot iron, then carefully separated the lace from the sleeve binding so that when she finished, the lace was as crisp as a brand new paper doily.

From the kitchen, their voices rose to a crescendo. Then a gunshot. Ellie ran and was approaching the wide door of the bedroom when Mr. Polk wheeled around and fired and fired again.

Hazel ran to the Polks' house and found Ellie, bleeding and struggling to pull herself toward the telephone. Hazel jumped over Mr. Polk, lying dead in the hall, and rushed to the kitchen where Miss Mattie, shot in the hip, slumped over the kitchen sink. It had all happened so fast, Hazel said. Mr. Polk wasn't in the house as long as he had sat in front of it.

I sometimes wondered if the measles might have saved my life. I could have been there playing jacks on the very same linoleum where Mr. Polk fell dead—could have been in the kitchen having a glass of milk with Sally and Miss Mattie, the unlucky survivor.

Ellie's death had happened to all of us, the whole town, and I felt like I had almost finished growing up. I was feeling the firsthand ache of other people. That happenstance thing came to mind again; somehow, without warning, you could find yourself in the way of your own Daddy's bullets.

July 6, 1943

Dear Dad,

This morning I received your letter of 19 June. The one in which you said you had just seen "The Road to Morocco." That is a hard road to travel and one that will be impossible for me to forget. I have heard that the picture had nothing to do with the real road to Morocco. I have not yet received any tobacco. Maybe it will come later as packages are not as fast as mail. There is no tobacco in this country at all. The Germans clean a place out completely. This place cannot produce tobacco and what there is of it here comes in from the Gold Coast and is rationed to the natives. The stuff is not good anyway. This place is very seasonal, it rained almost continually from the 1st of November to the middle of April. I have not seen a drop of rain since then. The valley we are camped in is now parched. Everything is dead. The wheat has been harvested and the stubble is as dead as can be. The only thing that is green are the pine trees. They are very hardy. This is a splendid country for hay. You asked about horses. They can be had for the asking. The most beautiful things you ever saw. They run loose and are very gentle. The Arabs are a wicked race, but they take good care of horseflesh. During the Battle of Mackenny, my company was some five miles from the rest of the Battalion and supply was quite a problem. Food, water and ammo had to be hand carried over four long miles of barren mountains. It was very difficult to walk over these mountains and almost impossible to hand carry enough supplies to maintain our ammo. I policed up 43 of these horses that were running loose and organized a pack train. Then a few men could care for our supply in great style. I carried so damn much ammo back into those hills that the Germans got the surprise of their lives. It was the last surprise of their lives as a matter of fact. These horses were also very good to carry our wounded and dead. For that little piece of work, I was awarded the Silver Star and received a battlefield promotion.

It was supply that made the success possible, but without fine horses it could not have been done. All of these animals are very tame and you can walk right up to one and pet him. About half of them are white and iron gray. You can ride any of them without saddle or bridle. All you have to do is get on him and lean over when you want to turn and when you want to stop, just pull on his mane. I will not say anything about military matters, except that we are training like mad. Yesterday I walked a mere 35 miles over very rocky paths. To be able to get from one place to another quickly is an important thing in the infantry. We will be in Africa only a short time now.

Where we are going I do not know but where ever it is, I am ready for it. I have the best company in the battalion. I can see that Capt. Walker was right. You must be firm to handle men in mass. I once thought it was heartless, but now I see that it is only a strong sense of responsibility. Well Dad, it has been 10 months since I have slept in a bed and over eight months since I have slept under a roof. It is very seldom that I get to sit in a chair or eat off of a table. I will know how to appreciate these things if I ever get the chance to enjoy them again.

It is very hard to be a good officer and at the same time hate this damn thing as I do. When I demonstrate a method of deploying our weapons to make them more deadly, I must act interested, but in my heart I hate it. I wish I could be myself for a little while—just say, "to Hell with it all" and walk off someplace. My boys are good soldiers and well trained and know how to carry out orders, but they are not happy and far from it. It has been a long time since I have heard them sing. They are very quiet. When they are told to do something, they do it without question and without thinking and I know that they are as unhappy as I am.

You write a lot about fox hunting. I appreciate it because you think that I like that. I did once, but no more. I know what it is to be the fox—to play a game when your life is the price for losing. Those stakes are too high for fun. I will never hunt anything. I will have no guns and set no traps. I have seen my friends blown to Hell with a booby trap. I will spend the rest of my life trying to forget it.

Please give my love and best wishes to all and hug Sari for me. I dreamed about her last night. She came running across the porch to meet me, but I had no arms to pick her up with.

Will write again soon,
Howard

5

A Time to Speak

The recital was postponed, and it was lucky for me because even with the extra time, I was not able to memorize the five pages, but ended up using the music in front of me. I rely so much on the notes anyway. I can sight-read almost anything—what my eyes see on the page seems to run through my fingertips to the keys. I never have to look down, but I can't add an extra chord, improvise, or change keys like my cousin Billy Earl, the paper boy.

This was the summer he and I started playing hymns together. I would play the hymns on the organ just as they were written, and he would follow me on the piano, adding runs and embellishing the notes just like they did at the Baptist Church. I had noticed this style of playing as I compared vacation Bible schools—went to all three, the Methodist, the Presbyterian, and the Baptist. The Baptist was the best. They had the activities that were the most fun to do and the most delicious refreshments, and they began their day marching in the sanctuary, carrying the flags, and singing "We've a Story to Tell To the Nations." I had heard Mama once call Baptist women "Wheelhorses."

I couldn't wait for Billy Earl to come by on his bicycle every day. After he ate some of Mama's leftover biscuits or crackling bread, we would start in on "Savior, Like a Shepherd Lead Us," then "When the Roll Is Called Up Yonder." Our finale was "Beulah Land."

⁂

It was Ruthie's year for the first fig of the season. Granddaddy brought it in with his usual ceremony, and we all watched as she savored the plump fruit and enjoyed her turn at being singled out. This ritual of Granddaddy's making always marked the official beginning of our summertime.

After our morning dairy chores, we played away the lazy afternoons—Sally, Mary Jean, Ruthie, and I marching up and down the long front walk playing wedding. Mary Howard was the flower girl, strewing flower petals in front of the bride. She held a little straw basket we had decorated with colored silk ribbons. The bride always wore Mama's torn white organza curtains pinned to her head with bobbie pins and needed two train bearers to keep the material from dragging the ground. We took turns being maid of honor, mother of the bride, and bride and then the groom, unless we could get Billy Earl to stand in when he could take time out from his paper route.

Granddaddy looked on from the front porch where he worked on his cane fishing poles—shellacking them and painting the corks with red fingernail polish so he could easily spot the first nibble of his hook. When he would let us borrow the fingernail polish from his tackle box, we would paint Mary Howard's toenails.

I was reminded that it was catawba worm season every time I went into the refrigerator for a drink of milk. The fish bait would always be there in the cigar box filled with cornmeal.

In between swigs of her energy jar of sweetening water, Josie peeled pears for canning, the whole kitchen now a steamy room of delicious smells. Ruthie and I escaped the heat and found relief on the front porch where we sat in the rocking chairs shelling butterbeans.

Like Brer Rabbit, born and bred in the Briar Patch, that summer I felt like I was "born and bred in the kitchen." I learned how things worked from beginning to end.

"Shoo that big un' over this way," said Josie, as I lunged after the Rhode Island Red. Somehow she grabbed the white one. All kinds of cackling and squawking went on all over the chicken yard. Feathers flew as she began ringing its neck. Even after the head was off, the chicken twitched and tried to stand up for a while just like it might have had a second life. Josie lay the limp fryer on the stump and chopped off the dirty feet. We went in the back door with the chicken, and I watched as Josie got the bird ready for frying. We dressed her, pulling out the feathers that had been loosened with boiling water. Josie emptied the gizzard of berries and corn, and I watched her cut up the chicken taking great pains to have a good-sized pulley-bone. She sat on her stool by the stove sipping her sweetening water and watched the chicken frying in the iron frying pan. She never left her spot, turning the pieces with her fork and putting more wood in the stove. Stirring the creamed corn we had grated earlier that morning, she told me how to add a little water along to keep it from scorching. I knew what the hoecake looked like when it was almost time to flip it over—stiff in the middle, crispy and brown on the edges.

"A couple o' pinches of sugar and 'bout three pods of young okra during the last fifteen minutes of cooking will help the butterbeans," Josie taught me. "And don't forget to add a little bacon grease." She whispered her secrets to me as she bent over the stove. I stood by her side, both our faces shining.

⁂

"Mama kilt me 'bout one lil' pear," sang Willie Mae as she jumped and turned around in the middle of the two jump ropes. Her mouth stayed full of something—snuff, camphor leaf stems, sugarcane. Her mouth moved all the time either chewing or chanting. She came up from the quarters to play with us sometimes on Saturdays. A high-yellow she was called and the best at jumping double rope.

Willie Mae told us about things we could never have learned from anybody else—Bloody Bones and Axe Murders. She would call up doodle bugs as we all squatted in the dark under the house. She would jab at the soft dirt mounds with a stick whispering, "Doodle Bug, Doodle Bug, fly away home, Your house is afire and your chiren' are all alone." Mary Jean and I turned the heavy dusty ropes, both our faces streaked with that bitter yellow liquid, Pete Strozier's eye water, warding off more sore eyes threatened by teams of swarming, darting gnats.

June 20, 1943

Dear Dad,

It is Sunday afternoon and I am sitting in my tent in the midst of a swarm of flies. I am writing with one hand and fighting off the flies with the other. It has been very hot today. This is a strange place, when it got hot, it did so very quickly. I love the heat and never complain about it. I am very happy to say that my mail is coming very good now. Last week I had a three day vacation. It was the first time I have had off since I reported for duty last August. I went up on the coast. It is very nice there. The Mediterranean coast is not at all like our coast, but is rock-bound. In some places, the mountains come right down to the sea. The sea is very calm and blue. It looks like I may see a great deal more of the Mediterranean before we are finished over here. We have a lot of equipment and supplies over here and are about ready for anything we may have to do. One thing is sure, we may be ready but I will not have my heart in any more operations. This damn thing of fighting is not good. Everyday I realize the effect of war on me. I will never be the same man I was. I have no faith in human nature and that is a bad thing. It would be nice if those who make wars had to fight them. Only then will there be no more wars. This place is very war conscious and when this one is over, there will be another one. I will not be in the next one. I suppose that you can tell from my letters that I am becoming a bit disgusted, that is true. I am very tired of the whole damn thing. I will continue on another sheet.

Howard

Granddaddy's wet shirt began to cling to his back, and you could plainly see the porous one-piece summer underwear he wore. The snip, snip of his clippers and fresh green morning smell of ligustrum competed with our little sticks as we stirred jars filled with fermented camphor berries, our "stink bombs."

"Let's wash up, girls," he said. "It's almost time for the noon train, and I'll bet that whistle's bringing us a letter. I want to get this one of mine down to the post office before the mail is wheeled to the depot."

June 27, 1943

Dear Dad,

This is the second of two letters. I hope you read them in that order. Letter No. One I wrote a week ago and figured that I would mail it when I wrote this one, but have been so pressed for time that I have been unable to write. We are training with such a degree of intensity that when I do have time, I am too tired. Last week I was on the go day and night. It seems that there is always something coming up to prevent rest. Enclosed is a paper that I wish you would save for me. It may be that I will need it some day. I am very proud to say that this promotion did not come through normal channels, but that I got it the hard way. Promotions are much harder to get over here than they are in the states. Why that is I do not know. A few weeks ago I thought that by now I would be on my way home, but I was bad wrong. I may be on my way soon, but not for home. Experience has shown that those who died in the early phases of the war are the lucky ones. I believe that they intend to fight this outfit to the last man—it would just be my luck to be him. Dad, you can see that your youngest son has changed. My heart is full of hate, I hate men. That is a terrible thing to say, but this is a man-made war. Do you remember how anxious I was to make a good officer? I did. I have often heard the statement that I am the best officer in the Battalion. I am no longer proud of it. It may be a long time before you hear from me again.

Howard

Cousin Sadie's daughter, Eunice, and our Cousin Willis will be married tonight at 7:30. He is an instructor in a group called "The Flying Fortress" at Sebring. Granddaddy says he is mighty lucky to be back in the States.

The ladies of the church have been bringing washtubs of flowers and putting them on the back porch. The wedding reception is at our house. Ruthie and I finished waxing the living room and dining room floors yesterday.

"Sari, put these newspapers down, in case somebody forgets and comes in the front door," said Mama. Josie is polishing the silver compotes for the nuts and mints, and Daddy just got all the prisms down from both chandeliers for Ruthie and me to wash. We are washing the borrowed little glass plates and stacking them in the dining room on the cutwork tablecloth Josie has just finished ironing.

Several members of Cousin Sadie's church circle are busy fixing huge bouquets in tall stand-up white wicker baskets for the front porch. Aunt Mamie and her bridge club are banking the mantelpieces with smilax and magnolia leaves, just like Christmas. The greenery will be the background for Mama's arrangements of gladiolus, white hydrangeas, and Queen Anne's lace.

"Ruthie, mold this chicken wire to fit this vase," said Mama, "just like you saw me fix this one. The wire will help me keep the bouquets loose and natural while supporting the tall stems," she explained.

Next she sent us outside to choose a few pieces of small ivy she needed to entwine among the silver candelabra on the bride's table. Ferns were brought in from all over the community, and now it was our last job to pick up any stray leaves or flower blossoms that had dropped on the floors.

The entire house smells of sweetheart roses, and I know when the reception is over, we can play wedding for several days using leftover flowers for our own procession.

The church was suffocating and filled to the balcony. As

I sat there I knew the ceremony order by heart and took my cue from the pianist when she changed keys and hit the first note.

The candles are lit—"O Promise Me"
Mother of the Groom arrives
Mother of the Bride arrives—"O Perfect Love"
Miss Thelma's Solo—"I Love You, Truly"
Processional March—"Mendelssohn's Wedding March"
The candles melt
The wedding vows—"To a Wild Rose"
Recessional March—"Mendelssohn's Wedding March"

I finished up my thirty minutes of piano background music for the reception; then Ruthie and I followed the guests next door to view the gifts. The living room, dining room, and entire sun porch were filled with tables from the fellowship hall covered to the floor with white sheets. We walked through the slow-moving line and saw each piece of Apple Blossom china displayed with the giver's engraved card there on the dish or under the piece of Chantilly silver. An extra shelf of white-painted tiers had been added to each table to take care of the shower gifts: pillowcases and sheets with crocheted edges and embroidered dish towels from the linen shower, assorted vases and serving trays from the miscellaneous one.

August 16, 1943

Dear Folks,

This will have to do for all so please circulate until I have more time to write to everyone. First off, I am well and unharmed. You are right. I am in Sicily, at the Eastern tip of it at present. I am very lucky. My company lost more men than any company in the regiment. We were in the toughest places. Our losses were much greater than those in Africa. It is strange to me that I am alive now. Many men have died on all sides of me and yet I am in good health. I had my glasses shot off of me. The bullet went through the lens and cut the frame in two and the only harm it did to me was nick the corner of my eye a little. To show you how lucky I am, in less than two days, I received the glasses from home. Maybe you will be interested to know that I have turned religious all of a sudden. I don't know just what kind of religion it is, but it is some kind—kind of a foxhole religion. There were many shells that hit close to me, but killed men further away and left me unharmed. There were three that made a triangle around me and a small triangle at that. Everyone that saw it clearly knew that I had been blown to Hell, but when the smoke cleared away, I came crawling out and other men further away were killed. That was the beginning of this religion. Somehow, I feel that my life must represent the lives of many others that have died. It could have been I as easily as them. From now on, I will be a better man. I am going to try to do somebody and everybody some good. I may never go to church, but I do have some kind of religion. Tell Lib that she can be thankful that she had no boy babies. I will write you again in about a week. Maybe I will know what is going to happen to me then.

With Love to All,
Howard

All during the summer, *The Richland Advocate* reported each week on the Social Page that the Bullard gardens were ablaze with color: "now blooming in riotous profusion." We waited each week for the newest description: ". . . guests to the Gardens will be greeted by a staggering array of Gloriosa Lilies flanked by a host of sweet peas and bachelor buttons."

The location of the "Gardens" was actually Miss Alma Bullard's side yard, really a thicket of vines and bushes and mostly orange gladiolus growing sideways to the ground. Nothing was planted in rows like Granddaddy's peas and onions. Stalks just cropped up; vines ran out of control up the fence and onto the porch. There had been no thought for tomorrow as far as growth—undergrowth or overgrowth—was concerned.

She could have taken some lessons from the field hands Granddaddy and I often watched as they used string to tie up the tobacco plants from their sand leaves (bottom leaves, often discarded) to the top of the shade. Then as the tobacco grew, almost every day they were out there wrapping the string around the stalk. Each leaf grew straight, tall, and orderly and was easily picked. Miss Bullard's marigolds and zinnias were choking and strained toward the sun from under a tree. It was as if she had come out on the back porch one moonlight night when all danger of frost had passed and had strewn seeds at random, which fell as slowly and unsurely as a dandelion's fuzz on her backyard jungle. It was hard for me to believe that a grown-up would blow things up to the point that facts were unrecognizable when reported in the newspaper. This kind of reporting was a little more than a step above Granddaddy's exaggerated hunting and fishing stories. I came to know that after you had sorted out the real truth for yourself about the things you read or heard as "chaff that the wind driveth away," there were more and more things that were not always as they seemed.

August 30, 1943

Dear Howard:

It's a fine, clear morning. Not too hot and may rain this evening. Most of the town will go fishing this afternoon as the stores close at 1:00 every Thursday. As yet we have not heard from you since you wrote on July 22 more than a month now. I do hope you are O.K. and that you are well and getting along nicely. The children are fine, but Mary Howard still wants my pipe and glasses. Helen (Mamie's daughter) is going to Miami to spend a week with Eileen before college starts. They talked over the phone and she says she has not heard from you for a month. Lib says she will look in the ice box and give you an inventory of some of its food today as we have lots of good things to eat.

Lots of Love,

Dad

"Fall is in the air, and Howard will be twenty-six next month," Granddaddy said one morning in September. We had already quit wearing our white shoes as we always did after Labor Day, and Mama had started sunning our wool clothes and blankets from the cedar closet. Daddy was laying in firewood. We could look forward to school days, and as Granddaddy loved to predict, "Fair and cool weather with very blue skies."

September 6, 1943

Dear Howard,

I am glad you are promoted to 1st Lt. and know you are a good officer and a good soldier however irksome it may be. I read over and over with interest and pride the way you worked the horses for a pack train for supplies. That in itself seems to call for more promotion. Wish I had one of those fine horses here—one that was in your pack train. Well, let us hope it will soon be over and we can all be together again. War is a pretty awful thing at best, but they forced war on us and we have to answer them in the only language they know—force and we will answer with a superior force. I enjoy your letters so much—the ones that tell of the country and how you get along with your men.

Write Soon,

Your Dad

P.S. Again, we are proud of your promotion.

Promotion Day at Sunday School was always around the last Sunday in September and just as reverent and significant as Easter. Our teacher made each one of us a certificate, and we all moved on to new classrooms. Ruthie, instead of bringing home the stiff pamphlet, "Beginner's Lesson Pictures," today held "The Primary Class," a loose-leaf two-page story with a memory verse and a "Something To Do" paragraph. Sometimes there was a song printed on the back that I could play for us all to sing:

"All things bright and beautiful /All creatures great and small."

A blank page was there sometimes for drawing pictures or to use for writing our own prayer. Anyway, I felt much older leaving behind the room with that familiar poster of Jesus surrounded by the children who came to see and hear him—the one where he is holding the smallest one. The inscription at the bottom we had said together many times: "Suffer the little children to come unto me."

September 18, 1943

Dear Dad,

First I will tell you about the tobacco you sent me. It was very good, but I only got two packages of it and have already eaten both of them. The glasses are also very satisfactory. By now you will know what happened to the pair I was wearing. It is now 8:30 A.M. and the men are engaged in preparing for an inspection. I will start my inspection at 9:00. I have a damn good company, Dad, and I intend to keep it that way. I sure learned a lot from Capt. Walker and if I had not, I could not fill the position I now have.

In your last four letters you said something about sending you a cable. Please let me enlighten you to the fact that I am a soldier in a war torn country where it is just as impossible for me to send a cable as it is for you to fly over here and visit me. Please do not mention a cable again. You should know better. Enough on that. Please forgive me for making a point over a trifle, but it was something that worried me.

About the cocola stock, I do not know much about it, but

I do not like any stock in a business of that kind even if it is a money making proposition. I wish you would look around and see what it will do in the way of providing a place to live. I would rather have that lot in front of Mose's house or maybe Kenon's house than all of the cocola stock there is. I intend to live there, you know. Please use your own judgement on that matter, but I do not favor cocola stock.

You people at home have been mighty good about writing. I want you to know that it has been a great help to me and seems to give me a reason for being here. I swear I would not fight this damn war for myself. By the way, I am not through fighting. The big run is just coming up. I hope my luck will continue to hold. I would give up tobacco for one year to see Sari for one minute. Tell her that I am coming home, and after I attend to a little job over here, I want her to come down to the train station and meet me.

I dreamed about Bert Watson last night. I dreamed that he came up to the house in his truck and asked me to go coon hunting with him. I asked him if he had a good coon dog and he said that the dog he had was not worth a damn, but that he had some good sausage that we could cook.

Love to all,

Howard

October 1, 1943

Dear Howard,

The headlines in today's paper states: THE DRAFTING OF FATHERS BEGINS TODAY. We have sent you chewing tobacco and Phillies. If you were here, we would have a pot of peas, pork sausage, fish-roe, cornbread and black coffee. Sari hugs my neck practicing so she can do a good job on yours. She is in a play depicting 1776 at the Women's Club today. You know how she likes that. We are catching a lot of speckled perch down at the lake.

Love,
Dad

My ruffled pantaloons showed as my hoopskirt swayed. I pointed my right foot and tapped it softly, moving toward my partner and then bowing. My pigtails had been coaxed into sausage curls at the back of my neck and I could feel them bouncing while dancing to "Minuet in G." Trying to concentrate on each changing pattern of eight movements, I kept listening for the F sharp that was a little flat. This was twice in one month I had been on the program at the Women's Club.

While accompanying Miss Delicia Oliver just a couple of weeks ago, I had played the snaggle-toothed piano with the missing ivories. Miss Oliver made a colored chalk drawing of her slow-forming landscape as I played the music set to Joyce Kilmer's poem, "Trees." Watching both the sheet music and artist tested me to wind up not long after she made her final, elaborate stroke.

30 September '43

Dear Dad,

At last it has happened, I had my picture made. I am very sorry that they turned out so badly. It was a very sunny day when they were made. I was commander of a convoy that was moving troops. It was the very first time that I have had an opportunity to get my picture taken so I made the most of it. The picture is misleading as I am much tanner than I look in the picture. Everyone tells me that I look very healthy—that is true. I am in very good health and enjoy eating anything I can get. My complexion is a deep ruddy and I am as hard as a rail. The men in my company swear that I am not human, but a machine built for speed and endurance. That is not true, however, as I am very human—more so than I have ever been before.

You ask me about the people here, they are a very low class of people—very dirty and their morals are very low. The island is over run with children and a lot of them do not have the proper identity. There will be a fine crop of young men here for the next war. These people seem to think that war is a national event. There are some beautiful natural harbors here. Mount Etna is the largest mountain on the island. I know just how big it is because I walked around three sides of it. The British 8th Army went up the east side of it and we went around the South, West and North side of it. I understand what Gibbons meant when he said, "Rome lost her power through her weakness."

The stock is run down in the same way as the people are. There are no beautiful horses here as there were in Africa. The Arabs were a very poor race, but they were a race and they had a plan to live by. These people over here have no plan. They just live. Sometimes I think it would be a very good idea if Mount Etna would erupt and destroy the entire island. The climate here is wonderful and the soil is very rich. There are some beautiful orchids and gardens here and could be many more if the people were not so lazy. These people will not work. They want to live without working. That is what caused the war. These people are very tired of the war and I think it rightfully so. They have paid a hard price. I frequently think of the old phrase, "Freedom is a hard won thing." One can understand that after having seen what I have seen. Ask Dink to tell you about the circus man who said that he was going to build a fence around his little place up in Georgia and raise dogs on it. I feel like I believe he felt.

I am getting plenty of mail from home now and I want you all to know that I appreciate it very much. I do not see how I could carry on if it were not for the letters I get from my wife. She is a very good writer. I realize more and more everyday what a mistake I made by not getting married when I was 19 years old. I have been much happier since the day I got married. Circumstances have made it a little hard on my wife, but then, maybe that is in the plan of things too.

By the way, I received two packages of chewing tobacco and one box of Phillies. I have eaten it all up long ago. You asked about my eye. It is undamaged. It was a very close call. I still have the frames of the pair of glasses that were shot off. The bullet cut the frames right in two, but did not touch me. My eye was cut by the glass but all of the glass was taken out and there are no scars left. I now have an oak cluster to wear in my Purple Heart. That shows that I have been wounded twice.

Maybe you could tell by my letters, that I have been very blue for the last month or so. I am in better spirits now. I shall try and write you a nice long letter this coming Sunday. I shall also send you another picture as this one may not reach you. I am anxiously awaiting the arrival of the pictures of you and the children. Tell Lib that I shall be disappointed if

I do not get a picture of my favorite sister-in-law. Other than my wife, she writes the best letters of all. Please give my love to all and assure them all that I am coming home. I am coming home to work, but first I plan a long rest. I need one badly. If the pictures of the children are not already on the way, please send them on. I have just finished writing to Mamie. I asked her to get some books for me. You can do me a great favor by giving her the money for them. They may be a little high, but the price can in no way compare with the pleasure I shall get from them. Tell Dink and Lib that I shall write to them both soon. When I try to write many things come into my mind—most of which I can not write. I have feelings in my heart that I know are not good and I have opinions that I shall never express. This I will say and stop at that. War is stupid. Maybe next Thanksgiving you and I shall sit in the sun and talk things over. Please give my love to all and if you will, help Mamie with the books.

Howard

What a friend we have in Jesus,
All our sins and grief to bear,
What a privilege to carry
Everything to God in prayer.

The deacons are still bringing in the folding chairs and placing them down the middle and side aisles of the church to accommodate the combined congregations. After the opening hymn, Aunt Mamie directs the choir, which competes with the men and then the women straining "The Awakening Chorus" into a sort of an echo.

There was another reason for these Fifth Sunday Night

meetings. Miss Daniels, the county health nurse, stood dressed in her crisp white uniform as she gave her report. Her presence here was just as scary as it was in the little sick room at school where she gave the typhoid shots. My arm grew heavy and feverish and in need of a sling just listening to her:

"And there were 42 cases of hookworm treated, 511 typhoid immunizations administered, and 22 home visits made during the month of October."

After a group of first graders recited the books of the Bible and the Twenty-third Psalm, Miss Cahill, the Bible teacher, made her appeal:

"We need volunteers to help with costumes and stage props for the Christmas pageant just a few weeks away. We need several large bathrobes and sandals for the shepherds and wise men, remnants of cloth or old sheets for head pieces. Any of you men handy with tools, we need you to reassemble the stable."

Aunt Mamie had already volunteered me again for the Virgin Mary, and I was again to wear Mama's dark blue tablecloth over my head—the same one she used to cover leftover Sunday dinner. The cloth would be all done up— washed, starched, and ironed and then placed over cold fried chicken, speckled butter beans, grated corn, pickled beets, stewed okra and tomatoes, biscuits, and cornbread with the bottle of pepper sauce and the syrup pitcher nearby. While the grown-ups took their Sunday afternoon naps, we would sneak and graze from the pickings underneath the soon-to-be-sanctified cloth.

As Miss Cahill spoke, she kept pushing her curdled upper arms into her tight short sleeves. The flowered handkerchief she wore in her blouse pocket kept reminding me of those pansy and morning glory stickers she gave out for memorizing a verse of scripture.

After the lay leader reminded us that the collection plate tonight "would help defray the expense of a Bible teacher for the school, thanks to the combined efforts of the churches," the Presbyterian minister gave the scripture reading. These verses always came before the sermon and were introduced as "appropriate." I noticed how Ecclesiastes 3:1-8 sounded like the poetry Granddaddy read to me except it didn't rhyme exactly. But it was so pleasing and musical to my ear that I could almost picture the words like notes and count the beats to the measure:

To every thing there is a season, and a time to every purpose under the heaven:

A time to be born, and a time to die; a time to plant, and a time to pluck up that which is planted;

A time to kill, and a time to heal; a time to break down, and a time to build up;

A time to weep, and a time to laugh; a time to mourn, and a time to dance;

A time to cast away stones, and a time to gather stones together; a time to embrace, and a time to refrain from embracing;

A time to get, and a time to lose; a time to keep, and a time to cast away;

A time to rend, and a time to sew; a time to keep silence, and a time to speak;

A time to love, and a time to hate; a time of war, and a time of peace.

—Authorized King James Version

I soon settled back into my usual church-going activity of planning the next dress I wanted Mama to make me. . . .

October 24, 1943

Dear Dink,

Now get set because, for good or bad, here comes "your long letter." First I shall thank you for the way you write to me. Yesterday I got ten letters—four from my wife, three from you, two from Dad and one from Mamie. It is Sunday morning and a very beautiful day. The sun came up like thunder out of Italy across the bay and it is just like a day in late October at home. Today I have little to do—just prepare myself for tomorrow's instructions and make my usual inspection of the men. I am sitting in the officer's tent now. I have just finished writing a thirteen page letter to my wife and shall use the rest of my spare time writing to you. The last letter of any length I wrote was the one to Dad. I wonder if he was able to read it? Yesterday was just another day with us. Things went on the same as always, but to me it was a milestone, my birthday. It has been a hard year, Dink. I have seen a lot of hard things come to pass and have been a party to a lot of unpleasantness. As a result of it, I am an older man. I know of a lot of things that are wrong and from it all I have learned many things. I have learned to have a deep sense of appreciation for little things. For instance, what a wonderful thing it is to be warm, to be able to rest when you are tired, to be able to sleep when you are sleepy. I have not learned a great deal about how to live with other people, but I know how to live with myself and that is something that everyone does not know. My relations with my men and my fellow officers are very pleasant. I am liked by both and it makes me feel very good. I feel that I am a good officer and that is a great reward. It is known that I have the best company in the infantry. Only yesterday the Colonel had all of his company commanders visit my supply tent and see how it is set up and then to make theirs like mine. My kitchen is by far the best and when some of the "higher ups" want a demonstration, they get me to do it for them. The men in the company know all of this and they are proud of it. The discipline in my company is very good. I shall have it no other way. I have a very fine group of non-commissioned officers in my company and they know that I am a hard man to fool. They do not try it anymore. So you see, Dink, I am getting along fine. I stay busy most of the time, but even then I am very homesick. Lib spoiled me, I guess and above all, I sure do want to see those little blue-eyed girls.

I think I shall send you one of my pictures, it is not a good one, but will do, I guess. I have cut off my mustache. I am in good health, but I can tell that I am not as good a man as I once was. Sleeping on the ground and taking all of the beating that I have in the past year has taken its effect on me. I do not sleep for more than a few minutes at a time and then I sleep very lightly. Not much like me, is it? My leg still aches me a little. I thought once that it was alright, but in the mornings it is a little stiff. I guess that is alright for the man that shot me paid a high price. His leg don't hurt him any though, I bet. Dink, sometimes let's go to Hickory Hill and camp on the bluff. Let's carry plenty to eat, make a lot of coffee with cream and fry some ham. Let's carry everything except gun shells and kind of talk things over. I cannot tell you what we are doing, but maybe in a few weeks you will know. When we do something it is big and makes wonderful news. I saw a paper from the States the other day. What do you think about the bastards that are striking? Boy. I would like to take "B" company over there with orders to round up those bastards and put them back to work. The coal would just fly out of the ground. I would make them dig so damn much coal that they would have to dig another hole to put it in. These things are very hard for a soldier to understand. The other day four of my men were caught up town with their sleeves rolled up. That is against regulation and the M.P.'s arrested them and they were fined $20.00 apiece. They were tried by a Summary Court. It cost me a hundred dollars and I was not even at the Court, but they were my men and I was responsible for them. Other than that, they had to answer to me for their conduct. I was not happy about them going against my orders and so I gave them one week hard labor under the 104 Article of War. "It is theirs not to reason why, theirs not to make reply. Theirs but to do and die."

So why the Hell should those bastards be allowed to strike? I am going to want to know that when I come home.

Do I owe my country more than they do? What is all of this free and equal stuff? Have the people back home gone crazy? What in the hell are we fighting for? These things are not for me to reason out, but, My God. I wonder about them. Do I have a right to live? Why me and not some of the boys at home get a crack at some of the rough stuff? Why in the Hell don't they hang Lewis? Why don't they kill a few thousand strikers, we have killed plenty of good men over here. Where are all the preachers (the ones with pretty watch chains that used to rock back on their heels and slam the rostrum with both hands and holler, "Thou shalt not kill.") What in the Hell are they saying now? Are they changing their tune and saying that God looks with compassion upon a soldier? Another thing, what about these men that write articles that run like this—"This must be an all out effort, a total war, a fight to the bitter end." Where is the man that writes like that? I'll tell you where he is, he is sitting on his haunches back in the States somewhere. Some of them say this, "We will fight to the last man." Who in the name of Hell is this "we" he writes about? I know who "we" is and he is not one of them. I have received many attack orders and he was not one of the men that went with me.

"To the last man." Think of that for awhile. Think of yourself as one of many men—dirty, wet, cold, and exhausted. It is just before dawn and you can see a long and high hill. You know that there are men there waiting for you. They are lying in slit trenches. They have many machine guns. Then, while you have a funny feeling in your stomach and feel kind of weak, you get the order—the order that you pass down to your men, maybe like this: "1st and 2nd Platoons, abreast,

4th at 0455, keep low, keep going and we'll reorganize on the forward side of the hill. Our direction of attack will be to the East."

Now, where are the grandstand quarterbacks? They want us to attack here, to make a landing there, sure, we will fight to the last man, yes, but not one of them has ever had that empty feeling that you have in your stomach, that weak feeling in the knees when an 88 just dropped in a hole you just left, or when you have just heard a few machine gun bullets whispering death near your ears, or when your friend, Joe Blow, over on the right of you just got his brains blown out by a 150 mm shell, or when you heard Pat Sack, over on the left, had his leg blown off at his knee start calling for his mother with such horrible screams, and then begging God that he might die to end his misery. Yes, we love our country. (But we hate some of the bastards in it.) We fight for it and if it is our fate, we will die for it. That is true love for one's country. What we hate are those bastards, those selfish bastards, in it. We hate those bastards that carry the banner down the streets and wave the flags on the 4th of July, on Armistice Day, and to see the soldiers off, then walk out and strike the very next day. Those are the bastards that are selling us short.

Yes, I know, they buy war bonds, war saving stamps. I know they turn in the old flat iron when the scrap man comes around. (They should, the bastards, they are making enough money to buy a new one.) The very next day they hoard a few pounds of sugar or snatch off a few extra pounds of meat. Sure, they are fighting bastards, when someone else is doing the fighting. Why don't we round them up? John L. Lewis included and send them overseas. Lewis would make a good yard bird for a latrine orderly.

Let them hear the drone of a Stuka's motor and the screaming of its siren as it releases its deadly eggs. Let them hear the chatter of the Messerschmidts machine gun as they rip up the dirt around them. Let them hear the whine of a bullet ricocheting around their heads. You can bet your life, they would be ready to dig then. Yes, they would dig deep. They would probably strike coal. You may rest assured that they would be ready to mine coal then, twenty four hours a day. It's a funny thing, but on the battlefield when the shells are falling thick and fast and the wounded are shrieking with terror, not a single man says, "I'll quit if I don't get $15.00 a day." They are fighting for their country, they love their country, it's for freedom, and they never strike. It doesn't take a lot of love for one's country to work eight hours a day, then go home to your wife and sleep in a soft bed. It does not matter if we sleep on the ground, and the wind driving a cold East wind in your face, if you go steady for three days and three nights carrying a three man load with no rest with Jerry taking pot shots at you along the way.

At night, when they put their feet under a table and enjoy a good meal (our boys have not eaten on a table for over a year), they pick up the paper and say, "Ah, our boys are certainly doing a wonderful job over there."

They can't read between the lines and see how much Hell the "Boys" caught that day. They did not know that the two miles gained that day was covered with blood of "our boys" over there. They did not know that John Doe, the boy that was mutilated that day had just become the father of a ten pound baby girl that day, one that he has never seen, one that he never shall see. Sure, they are fighting bastards, as long as some one else is doing the fighting. This is what we think of them over here.

Well, Dink, I told you to get set, you have been asking for a long letter for a long time and now you have one.

Well, I have had my say, now you have yours.

                                    With love to all,
                                    Your brother

                                    1319 Meridian Avenue
                                    Miami, Florida
                                    December 27, 1943

Dear Mr. Charlie:

Thank you a million times for the check. It was certainly sweet of you to send it.

The last I heard from Howard was about three weeks ago. The letter was postmarked about the twentieth of November and he was still in Sicily. However, he also sent a Christmas card on which he said that I wouldn't be hearing from him for quite a while. The people who live in the apartment across the way from us have a brother who is also in the Ninth Division. They've received a letter from him from England and I'm quite firmly convinced that Howard is there now too. I've heard that Patton is there and I feel quite sure that Howard is with Patton's Seventh Army. As soon as I get a letter from him, I'll wire you as I know how anxious you must be feeling about him. I try not to worry about him, but it's a job keeping my chin up especially at this time.

Our Christmas wasn't too happy a one as mother is still quite sick. We went through quite a siege with her, but I guess I can safely say, she is out of danger now. She is back from the hospital, but still in bed where she'll have to stay for at least two more weeks.

I feel sure that both your Christmas and ours was a great deal happier than last years. I pray that next year we'll have Howard back with us. Somehow I feel it will be before next Christmas.

Thank you again, Mr. Charlie, for being so grand to me. Give my love to C.B., Elizabeth, and the girls and thank them for me for their nice card.

Much love to you,

Eileen

⁓❦⁓

Granddaddy read from *The Once and Future King:* "'The best thing for being sad,'" replied Merlin, beginning to puff and blow, "'is to learn something. That is the only thing that never fails. You may grow old and trembling in your anatomies, you may lie awake at night listening to the disorder of your veins, you may miss your one and only love, you may see the world about you devastated by evil lunatics, or know your honor trampled in the sewers of baser minds. There is only one thing for it then—to learn. . . . Learn why the world wags and what wags it. That is the only thing which the mind can never exhaust, never alienate, never be tortured by, never fear or distrust, and never dream of regretting. Learning is the thing for you.'"

As I watched the reflection of the fire splayed on the ceiling there in Granddaddy's bedroom, I noticed Ruthie nodding in the big overstuffed chair, clutching her new Christmas doll.

A Time to Speak   111

It was funny how and what people chose to learn, I thought. Take, for instance, Billy Earl. I knew the notes, but he knew the music. Ruthie wasn't even interested in taking music lessons, but she and Daddy, both with a real knack for math, couldn't wait for Uncle Howard to send them a challenging problem. They all like things neat, precise, and working to perfection. Uncle Howard used to tease Daddy about walking in a room and first closing all the doors, then straightening all the picture frames.

England
December 23, 1943

Dear Dink,

It is not within the limits of words, my words, to tell you how happy I was to get your nice letter. For a few minutes while I was reading it, I was transfigured. I was no longer an army officer in a far away land, but just an ordinary man at home.

I cannot tell you a great deal about the people here as I have not seen very much of them. The country is very beautiful. Every farm here looks like maybe it belonged to Mr. Tom Cook. You know what I mean, don't you? The stock is of the very best and in good shape. The fences are built to stay and the gates will open and shut.

These people take great pride in their homes and keep them up. They have more time than we do for things and another cause is they do not have as much gasoline as we do. You should see the way they stack their hay—it would do your heart good. They stack it up like a corn crib, bigger at the plate than at the sills, then fix it up like a gable and put a

thatched roof on it. Of course, all of this is only hay, but I believe that if the farmer who did the work had a good car
and plenty of gas, he would have less hay. The horses used
here are the big heavy kind and the harnesses are a pleasure to look at.

This morning I went on a march (by the way, I was acting
Battalion Commander) throughout the country. You would
have enjoyed it—just a little twelve mile march which we
made in two hours and forty-five minutes. There was a heavy
frost on the ground all morning. I could not help but enjoy it.
My company went on guard this afternoon and so I am the
Officer of the Day. That, of course, means Day and Night.

It is now 7:05 P.M. and everything is going along smoothly
as it always does with me for I will not have it any other way.
Everyone here knows that B Company is the best outfit of
them all. As bad as I want to come home, I would not leave
my men over here and return if I had the chance. I just now
took time off and read your letter again. I must say that I did
not know you had it in you to write a letter like that. The men
in my company say I am too mean to die, but I am afraid to
be shot at anyway. No story or newsreel can ever give you
an idea of what a Hell of a thing this is. Well, there I go getting off on the wrong things again. It makes me feel good to
think that something that I wrote you made you think as I do.

You know, Dink, we are very different in a lot of ways, you
are musical and I cannot whistle, but I can recite from
memory more poetry than you ever read.

There are many things that I could point out to show that
we are not alike, but there are many more things that we
have in common. The older I get, I feel that the nearer I fly
back to the family block. You said you notice little things.

When I get home I am going to find out many things. I am going to study. There is just so much I don't know. Never before have I had so strong a desire to learn more about the things I wonder about now. What is electricity? What is magnetism? What is gravity? How does the sense of taste work? What is light? Why does a magnetic field attract a conductor when a current is flowing through it. How does mental telepathy work? Why does a hog "tote straw" when the weather is fixing to turn cold? What is the square of 1? Why does a top roll backwards when it stops spinning? Why does a light shine through a fat shingle? What is fire? What is space? Why does a piece of iron turn red when it gets hot?

It makes me feel sad when I realize how little I know. I also feel frightened when I realize how much there is to know. Tell me, why is it that young men sometimes die while old men live? You see, there is no end to the things that we see that can stand a great deal of thinking about. You can talk to me, Dink, but you cannot understand me. I have seen too many things that you have not seen for you to understand me.

When I come home, I will be a man without a country. You see, I have become a part of these things. Did you ever hear a big mountain firing in the distance and know that you were the target? Then about fifteen seconds later hear the whistle of the shells? You can't see them, but you know they are coming. They sound louder every second and the seconds become minutes. After you hear them scream for about twenty seconds, they hit. Maybe on all sides of you. You do not know if you are hurt or not. About that time you hear the mountains firing again. No, that never happened to you and may it, please God, that it never shall. What God?

The one that stands by and lets this sort of thing happen? That is another question—maybe you can answer that one.

I know, Dink, I have not been writing as often since I have been here as I did in Sicily. I shall try to do better, I cannot complain about my mail. No complaint, but a request—ask sister-in-law to write. She is the best of all. Every time I get some V-Mail I try to rip the cover off to see who it is from and am just a little disappointed that I have not heard from the old "ice-box" in the last few weeks.

I haven't given Christmas a great deal of thought. Do you remember the Christmas I fired the cap pistol up the fireplace? Last Xmas I had a 45 automatic around my waist. This Christmas, what?

I have before me the pictures of your three little girls. I would like very much to hold them in my lap. My eyes get kind of watery when I look at the picture of the little one. My! how I would like to hold her in my hands, the same hands that have used a trench knife, that have taken lives. You may say that I am a master killer, because my work is to lead men in battle. What will she think? I have killed and death of any other name is the same. It is not good to write like this and I know it but why hide it. I am going to have to face it the rest of my life. I shall not be home until the war is over, then I cannot leave it. I shall carry it with me like an albatross* the rest of my life. The only answer is to find my true place in the plan of things.

I can't help but feel I did my wife a great injustice by marrying her, for I shall not come back the same man that left. She tells me that she understands and that everything will be all right and maybe she is right. I am going to try awfully hard to make good.

Will you help me make and fly a box kite? Sometimes let's take about four days off and do some real kite flying. I hope you understand this letter. You see, I am thinking of a lot of things that I do not know how to write. When I finish this log to you, I shall not write any more for about a week, so please let this suffice for all. Give my very best wishes to everyone. I believe you can understand how it is very difficult for me to write. There is nothing I can say. If you were here I may be able to talk to you, but I just cannot write. When a man writes there is only one view expressed and for about the same value of a person talking to himself. Maybe I am just using you?

> Love to all,
> Your brother, Howard

*ask Mamie

All dressed up, I leaned my head against the velvet sofa and was careful not to crumple the bomber pillow, I called it. It was from the Philippines and was a bright yellow with airplanes on it and MOTHER painted across it and some words underneath. I didn't want to put it in my lap and straighten it to read them. I just kept stroking the deep yellow fringe and thought how the sleazy material looked just like those dresses on the dolls you could win at the medicine show.

It was the first New Year's Day I had gotten to celebrate by going to Aunt Cliff's eggnog party. The silver punch bowl on the coffee table held the brew, topped by a meringue-whipped cream glob. Impossible to eat or drink without leaving a foamy mustache on your upper lip. I tolerated it, just for Granddaddy's sake. I managed to swallow a little bit between mouthfuls of dried apple cake and some toasted pecans from one of the candy dishes nearby.

Back of the bar, in a solo game, sat
Dangerous Dan McGrew
And watching his luck was his light-o'-love
The lady that's known as Lou.

Granddaddy's nephew, Dan, recited. Dressed in his Air Force uniform, he was back in the States now, one of the lucky ones, and maybe home for good. As I listened to the rest of the poem, I pictured the special Holiday Greetings, the front of a special card we had received only a few days before:

Dear Dad,

This will have to do for all as I can send only three. I sent one to Mamie and one to my wife. I am reminded of the grief I must have caused you last year and I hope you shall have a better Christmas this time. It looks like maybe I shall have a White Christmas. Please give everyone my best wishes and fool Sari on a present from me. Make it appear that it came through the mail.

It is likely that my Christmas will not be merry, but I am a great believer in the New Year. Maybe it holds many good things in store for us all. With this card I am sending my love to all.

Howard

6

A Time to Keep

Granddaddy let me help him send some books today: *The Rubaiyat of Omar Khayyam*, the Edward Fitzgerald Translation, Thompson's *Trigonometry for the Practical Man*, *Strength of Materials* by James E. Boyd, and *The Last of the Mohicans*. I recognized James Fenimore Cooper's name from my author cards. As I helped Granddaddy get them ready, the package seemed even more precious than the tobacco we had sent several times before. We drove down Main Street past Spooner and Morgan, the combination grocery and dry-goods store where I could go and look through Simplicity Pattern Books with Mama and where I always wished I could ride the tall ladder on wheels they used to reach the shoe boxes stacked to the ceiling. We parked across the street at the post office and took our package to Miss Emma at the front window. After waiting there a little while, Granddaddy and I followed Bly Whipple as he pushed the two-wheeled wooden cart loaded with the bags marked US MAIL down the block to the depot. This brown and yellow building was next to the Planters Exchange, which backed right up to the railroad tracks where ingredients for their "Tobacco Special" fertilizer were unloaded directly from the box-cars. Standing with Granddaddy as the train pulled slowly away, I waved to the conductor until the caboose was out of sight.

England

January 10, 1944

Dear Mamie:

One purpose of this is to show you how a Xmas card may be used. When I think of my sister sending me a card over 3,000 miles of ocean and many miles of land and the entire message is "Lots of Love, Mamie," I cannot help but laugh. I was a very homesick boy when I got your card. After I got it, I was mad as Hell. As you can see, it is possible for a person to write a complete letter on the front and back and on top of the printed messages of words such as "Greetings and Best Wishes for the Christmas Season and the coming Year." And what is the significance of the big ship on the front and the printed phrase by Whitman? "The port is near/the bells I hear/The people all exulting."

Did you think that an old custom had you under obliga-tion? You are not. You may write only when and if you want to. Please rest assured that I will be very glad to hear from you but you do not owe me anything.

You may well ask, why don't I write? I will tell you. I do not have time to write. I have nothing to write about, except that any day may be my last and in the meantime, I would like to hear from my sister.

I received reports on Thanksgiving Day from Dink and the rest of my folks at home. They all wondered where I was and how my Thanksgiving was spent. I was at sea. Somewhere far up in the North Atlantic Ocean. It was a very windy day and cold, the sea was rough and I was plenty homesick. I could remember many Thanksgiving Days. They kept going through my mind all day. I thought of the hot, smoked sausage from the most recent hog-killing, all that dressing and gravy—of women unpacking their baskets, then packing them back up after dinner, of the river being low and maybe the children wading out to the sandbar, of old Gadsie pouring coffee she had made earlier over the fire, her black hands so chapped they looked almost white. I thought of you, Mamie, watching over the Book. Also I was reminded of my last Thanksgiving Day. About all I had to be thankful for then was that I was a better shot than the other fellow was. Since then, however, I have wondered just which one of us came out of that deal the best.

I am going to send you some money in a few days. I won $1,000 dollars last pay day. When I get somewhere where I can buy money orders I am going to send them to you. Please carry them to the bank and buy $25.00 War Bonds. Leave them at the bank for safe keeping. I would rather only you and I knew about this. If I have been too hard on you about the Xmas card deal, please forget it. I won't. Maybe you did think I would like the poem on the front.

Give my love to all and tell them that I will come home. I
don't know when, but I will. I have plenty of blood on my
hands now and I intend to do a good job while I am at it.

Lots of love,

Howard

I toasted my legs and toes in front of the fire, then
tucked my sock-covered feet inside my long flannel night-
gown. I felt like I was in a cozy, warm tent. When I sat
resting my head at the foot of Granddaddy's chair and
stared into the fireplace, I again imagined the characters
he described and actually pictured them moving and
dancing there on top of the spitting, hissing logs.

I saw Brer Fox, Brer Bear, and the Tar Baby and heard
Brer Rabbit's high, jeering voice. Granddaddy chuckled as
he changed his voice and dialect to give life and definition
to the characters we had all grown to love.

Ruthie snuggled on one side of his lap. Mary Howard
kept knocking off his glasses and playing with his hair as
she fought the idea of settling down. Soon even she was
quieted by the rhythm of his voice as he began with the
poems that were easy for me to recite with him now:

> Week in, week out, from morn till night,
>   You can hear his bellows blow;
> You can hear him swing his heavy sledge,
>   With measured beat and slow,
> Like a sexton ringing the village bell,
>   When the evening sun is low.

Week in and week out, there in Granddaddy's room

(inside his castle wall) in front of the fire it was as if we had stepped inside the poem, "The Children's Hour."

From my study I see in the lamplight,
  Descending the broad hall stair,
Grave Alice, and laughing Allegra,
  And Edith with golden hair.

Mary Howard was asleep now, a strand of blond hair stuck to one nostril coated with Mentholatum.

"Tell us the story of Wiley and the Geese," begged Ruthie. It was our favorite. It really had no plot, but there was something about the way he told it. His food descriptions could set my mouth to watering. I could just hear the geese cackling as the little boy, Wiley, chased them, causing all kind of commotion among his Mama's backyard Sunday company.

Granddaddy continued to spit tobacco juice into the fire, but missed, and the brown liquid sizzled on the tile hearth like grease on a hot hoecake griddle. Tobacco juice leaked into the wrinkles on either side of his mouth, and the crevices looked like the little rivers or tributaries we were studying in geography.

"And so if that ole rabbit gentleman don't lose his barber pole crutch, I'll tell you the story tomorrow night of Uncle Wiggly and the Bad Boy," he finished. I carried Mary Howard across the hall into our bedroom with the three little iron beds lined up against the wall just like

Goldilocks and the Three Bears. As I slid between the icy sheets, huddling and trying to keep in the warmth I still had from the fire, I could hear Granddaddy moving about. From the rustling sound and the distinct smell coming from underneath his bedroom door, I knew he was crushing and mixing his tobacco leaves on the empty single bed in his room. Tomorrow his closet would be full of his special mix of Prince Albert, Beech-Nut, Sir Walter Raleigh, and some leaf tobacco from the Wayside Farm.

January 24, 1944

Dear Howard:

Well, we have killed the hogs and sure have some nice meat—150 lbs. sausage, 100# nice white lard, lots of ribs and back-bone and several sides of bacon. I pickled some pig feet and sure wish you could have some of them. We are well-fixed for food. We have pretty weather now. At night on the porch in the moonlight, I bet you could read a newspaper. I'll write again in a few days. Until then, wishing you lots of good luck. So long.

Your brother,
Dink

January 30, 1944

Dear Howard,

January is nearly gone and we are having fine clear weather and do wish you could have some of these days over there or do you? Do you have lots of fog and rain? Have you been able to go around a bit to see the town and people and do they talk like Robert Burns reads? They are noted for their cunning and thrift. Are there wild pheasant on the Moors? Of course, there are not wild turkeys there. Is it very cold there and how long are the days? Wish I could be with you and be fit to do the things you have to do. I feel so tied down when there is so much to do to win. At seventy-four, I am feeling my age. We are all well. Dink has not gotten his call yet but expects it soon. The canning factory has enlarged and are now dehydrating as well as canning. They are putting out lots of food for the Army. Hope you get some.

I have to read several books a night with two and sometimes three little girls on my lap at one time, but I like it.

Your Dad

"Hold it still," Mama said as she began melting the one pink candle. I held the white enamel pan upside down and steady on the big cake plate. In the center of the overturned pan, Mama stuck the candle in its little melted puddle. She put pansies all around the chipped red-rimmed edge like she always did with a real birthday cake.

Ruthie and Daddy had Mary Howard outside ready to pose for her birthday picture. As Daddy lined up the Brownie Kodak, Mama and I eased the cake with its "perfect white icing" onto the little table in the backyard and lit the lone candle. After we sang "Happy Birthday" to Mary Howard, Ruthie and I stood beside her—all three smiling into the February sunshine.

ری

March 3, 1944

Dear Howard:

Nearly two months now since you wrote. We are anxious about you. Can't think of anything to keep you from writing unless you are sick or injured or in a hospital somewhere. If so, get a nurse to write. You can't blame us for wondering what is the matter with you. The house is full of camellias and pansies and Lib is fixing flowers for the church tomorrow. The geese have gone North, the lawn is green. Dink mowed for the first time today. So Spring is a fact. Sari sends love.

Your Dad

March 14, 1944

My "dear ole brother-in-law,"

Did you know your ole sister-in-law has decided you have struck me off your list? Don't make me feel like that, heah me? You're right on the top of my "brother-in-law list"—les you do better about writing me I might put you down a notch or two. I'm teasing. No other "brother-in-law" of mine will ever get your place—even if you do put ashes on the floor and in my lap. But couldn't you send me a little word every now and then? We all celebrate when we hear from you. Here lately you've sorta neglected us. I'd write more often but all the others are writing and I feel like they tell you everything. I'm just an old sister-in-law and if I'd say the wrong thing, you'd never forgive me. I love to write to you tho'. I wish so much you were here to see Mary Howard.

Dink hasn't had time to fly a kite. The weather is beautiful for kite-flying, also fish-frying. Also Ochlocknee is all over the woods now. We have been to the woods on our Spring ride as usual. Mr. Charlie's turkey tales keep varying. Put me back on your list 'cause you're on the top of mine. I have lots of little things to tell you.

Lots of love,
Lib

They had all been acting kind of jittery, but finally we got word.

February 2, 1944

Dear Dad,

Thanks very much for the good letter writing you have been doing. I enjoy your letters very much but I just cannot write. I am well and strong. Please forgive me, I know that you nor anyone else cannot possibly understand why I do not like to write. If I wrote the things that are in my heart I would be tried for treason. When I write the things that are not in my heart, I hate myself for it. There is so little that I can say and the things that I can say you would not be interested in. I am an Army officer and that is as far as I go. I have the best company in the United States Army and am very proud of it. I am getting along good with my men and officers. I never go anywhere except in the line of duty. I have been to London twice. Perhaps you wonder why I am not a captain by now. I have been doing a captain's work for a long time and doing it good. I, too, sometimes wonder about that. Most of the ratings go to some hollow-head back in the states. Please do not ever think that maybe I am not doing my job. I am—and doing it well.

It is getting more and more difficult for me to write. You see, when I write I think of home and I am not so sure that I shall come home again. I have drawn many lucky cards from the deck in the past and I feel that this time my number is coming up. This is a dangerous affair we are faced with and it looks like we are going to see a great show over here. I am not fooling myself.

You can tell Dink that I received his telegram in three days but did not reply. We use that means of communication only in an extreme case. I shall write Lib soon. Tell her I know 57 ways to fix Spam. Hug all the girls for me and give my love to all.

I would love to raid your closet.

Howard

"Howard's always insisting that the only way to have enough gravy is to funnel it down from the attic through a hose hanging over his place at the table," Mama laughed as she put one of his old letters back in her apron pocket. It was that little bowl of fish grease gravy she fixed for Chance Williams on Saturday nights that convinced me that the way to make a man feel really special was to make a dish especially for him and put it by his plate before he even looked around for it.

Chance was always dressed in a blue chambray work shirt, black pants, black coat, and a black hat just like the hillbillies in the Lil' Abner cartoon in the funny papers. Ruthie and I never could tell if his hair was blonde or gray, but we knew he was old and one of the few men left in town. His eyes were crossed and he never said a word. I don't know how Mama ever found out he liked fish grease gravy. Every Saturday we would have our mullet and grits early because Chance had to walk several miles from the country, and he needed to be through in time to see the double feature before his brother-in-law, Bert Vickers, would close his meat market and take him home.

Ruthie and I had heard he lived in his sister's attic. "Saturday is Chance's only day of independence," Mama said. "He would never be allowed to stop and eat with us unless our house was directly in line with the Leaf Theater. So, you girls, don't stare; just eat and talk quietly among yourselves."

And because Granddaddy had usually taken us to the 1:30 matinee, I wondered about some things as we ate mostly in silence. "Think of the other fella," Granddaddy would often remind me. I wondered if Chance caught his breath when that sudden rush of popcorn aroma greeted him as the double doors to the narrow lobby closed behind him. I could picture that lone figure in black under the balcony and wondered if he ever laughed at the jokes of Frog or Gabby. Did he notice that the horses passed the same rock, the same tree, while they chased the bad men? Could he follow the bouncing ball? Did he inch a little forward in his seat when the Indians came up over the hill? Was he afraid like me, afraid of the MGM lion, the biggest cat of them all? When they showed the serial, did he look forward to next week when the believable explanation would be revealed? Would he be able to understand the last-minute escape? I tried to put myself in his shoes, those brogans that knew only the way to our house and the Saturday afternoon picture show.

March 15, 1944

Dear Howard,

Let me tell you about yesterday. First of all, it was a beautiful day, just like a spring day. We all got up just a little after sun-up and had a good sausage breakfast and played with the children and helped get them ready for Sunday School and then Papa carried them, and when they got back Elizabeth and I went to church. When we got back we had a good chicken noodle dinner, dressing, gravy, corn bread and ice cream. I talked about how I knew you would have liked to be here with us and the noodles, everything was so good.

After dinner, I got the little red wagon, and put a wide board across the sides to make a seat for Mary Howard to sit on. Sari and Ruthie walked close beside her. We went all down by Mose's house and around by the school house and you can't know how happy they were, as well as myself. I would tell Mary Howard to sing and she would try to do it. Every time she saw somebody, she would wave and say "Hi-Dah". She sure is some sport.

When we got through with this, we went in the garden to see if the fruit trees were living, and every one of them had little leaves and two of the peach trees had a bloom. I am sure proud of them and hope that we will all get to eat some of their fruit. After this, Elizabeth served coffee on the porch and we watered the flowers, had supper and put the children to bed, and then she and I went to church. I had such a good time, that I just wanted to tell you about it.

I will let you know how I come out if I am called to Blanding. I am going to ask for the Army.

Your brother, C.B.

๑๕๖

It was dark when we left the house, but we could see fairly well because of the moonlight. I sat in the back seat, Daddy and Granddaddy in the front, on our way to the corner store where we were to meet the other fox hunters. Most of the hunters had trucks with special cages for their dogs. When we met, we followed them to Hickory Hill. All helped build a fire as the dogs were turned loose yelping and sniffing in the tall grass.

We ate ham and eggs cooked over the fire, and the men just sat around on the bean hampers and listened to the dogs. "Listen to Old Bessie," one said, "she's in fine tune tonight." "She's making beautiful music all right," said another. A whole chorus of dog baying filled the damp morning air. "They must've treed 'em," said Granddaddy as he kept on whittling.

A little after sunup, the hunters called the dogs in, loaded up and we headed for home. Because of the moon,

I didn't even get to see that phenomenon I had looked forward to—foxfire, that eerie phosphorescent light Daddy had told me about that is given off by decayed wood on a dark night.

So much for fox hunting.

April 14, 1944

Dear Howard:

Dink and I put out some lines in the creek and got one fine fish and put out more lines today and hope to get some tomorrow. My garden is nice. We will soon have beans and potatoes. We have turnips, onions and carrots now. So hope you will come and help us eat so many good things. Lib says she will fix just the things you like. The children are too young to worry too much, but Sari is broken up. She does not say much but wonders what it is all about. Nearly all the young men are gone now. Only a few left and there is another call on June 1st. We will get on O.K. We are all well and I have taken off one of my sweaters, so you know spring has come, but it's still cool at night and early morning. Wish you could see the house so pretty. The azaleas and white spirea are in full bloom, the wisteria on the pecan tree is blooming and the pansies in the ring by the front steps are the best we have ever had. The lawn is green and the trees are all green and people say its such a pretty place. Write when you can.

Love,

Your Dad

March 2, 1944

Dear Dad,

Today is truly a beautiful day. The sun is shining and birds are singing. Today is the first good day I have had since I have been in England. There are no blooms yet, but I am told that Spring comes mighty fast once it starts. It is cold but very clear. I just saw a large force of flying fortress pass over. It is a beautiful day to beat Hell out of Germany. The cigars came about four days ago and the leaf came yesterday. I am well fixed for chewing now.

There are very good people here. I have some good friends here that I shall never forget. If I ever have a son, I shall send him over here to go to school. You would enjoy a trip here in the summertime. I am told that the days are 22 hours long during the last of June. They sure were short in December.

I have met several Scotch people and they are all good. They strike you as being honest and hard working farmers. It was difficult for me to understand them at first. It was like the first time you read "To A Mouse." There are several different dialects. Some of the Scotch from the mountains wear funny looking clothes. You can see a lot of skirts and kilts among them. There are no Irish here. They are not so well liked around these parts. I was out on the moors yesterday. It was cold and windy there. I have seen a few blossoms and I think that things will be green in about two weeks. All of the ground is well broken and ready for planting. These are good and thorough farmers with good stock. Most of the fences are made from a hedge that is very neat. Their haystacks are neat and everything is clean. A meat shop here is as clean as a beauty parlor at home. The more I am around this country, the better I like it. They are good people. The winter is all that is wrong here. I am feeling fine and will write to you again very soon.

With love,
Howard

Wed., March 8
England

Dear Dink,

First I shall thank you for the nice five page letter. It was the best yet. Your description of my boy Holly was pretty close. He is from South Carolina, about 20 miles from Augusta, Ga. The rest you were right about. He is no longer with me. I had him reclassified and transferred. He has seen a lot of this war and I did not think he could stand another campaign. When he left he had tears in his eyes and I did not feel much like laughing myself. He is much better off where he is now, but I shall miss him. I have a new man now and I do not know where any of my equipment is. Every time I want something, I have to look for it. I think Holly spoiled me, in fact, I am sure of it. He will write me soon as he promised to keep in touch with me. Someday the three of us will go camping together.

Do you remember when I was in Africa, I was on the colonel's staff for awhile. I am back on it now. I have been released from "B" company, but the new assignment is only temporary. I am now S-4. If you do not know what that means, ask some soldier. It is a good job and I know how to handle it. It also gives me more spare time and that is the reason I have been doing more writing in the past week or so. I am very glad to be on the colonel's staff. He is a good man and I think the smartest man I ever knew. He is a West Pointer and he can see through a stone wall. A commander of troops does not pick officers for his staff that he does not have confidence in. I shall do my best because I like him very much. I am sure that later when the going gets hard and we have a piece of ground to take that Jerry does not want to give up, he will send me back to "B" Co.

I am sitting in a nice warm office beside a heater. The sun is shining outside and the day is as clear as a bell, but still no sign of Spring. To sit here and look outside you would think it would be nice and warm, but there is ice out there.

This certainly is a beautiful island with a lot of good people on it. I think it is a shame that it could not be moved about 2,000 miles South of here. I have some good friends here that have been very nice to me. The way they ask me to come see them is they call me up on the phone and say, "We have a good fire tonight, come on over and have a foot-warming." I will sit by their fire and toast for a few hours. I usually leave here after dark with my overcoat on and then I do not have to put on my dress clothes. That makes it very convenient.

Last night I dreamed of you, Lib and Mamie. Lib said that I could sit on her bed and eat a piece of watermelon if I wanted to. Mamie said that she had some good noodle soup. That put such a strain on me until I woke up and missed it all. I tried to go back to sleep and continue where I left off, but something else happened and I was side-tracked to Sicily. I suppose that I shall have many dreams about Sicily, but maybe in time they shall grow dim.

Received the books the other day. I have been doing a little studying each day since I have been here. Maybe in a year or so I will know how to work fractions. About the only way I can rest is to get interested in a problem of some sort. I find it gets more and more difficult for me to keep my mind on one thing for a long time. I once had fairly good control of myself that way, but not anymore. It is hard to feel that you are slipping. It is not a pleasant feeling at all and I am definitely slipping. That is the reason I said that we would go up to Hickory Hill sometime and think things over. About six months ago I thought that when the war was over, I would live a quiet, easy life and just let the rest of the world go by.

After you see a lot of men die you begin to say, "What in the name of Hell are we fighting for?" or "Is it worth it?" I do not know what we or anyone else is fighting for, but I do know that it isn't worth it and I am going to make some of those people at home pay off and do it good. I am getting so damn tired of hearing this damn thing about "fighting for your country, for freedom, for liberty, for democracy," or anything else. The way they (the generals) put it up to us is something like this. "You men have been selected, yours is the privilege to fight to defend your loved ones." Sometimes I may jump up and say, "Defend them from what?" The Germans are defending their loved ones also. My God, but this is a stupid war made by a lot of heartless men and women.

Let me ask you a question. What do you know about the Germans? By God, I am proud to say that I have German blood in me and if that is treason, then make the most of it. I am sick of the whole damn thing, but I am too little to stop it. I will go on, I will do my best. I hate it and always shall. If it is such a Hell of a great privilege to be where I am, why don't they give someone else a chance. I wear eight medals now and that is a Hell of a lot more than I wanted.

Well, well, my mail orderly just looked me up and gave

me two V-mail letters. That sure was a good dinner you had. You see, I have had noodles on my mind and that makes it worse. I can just close my eyes and see noodles and chicken, in fact I don't have to close my eyes to see them.

I still cannot believe that you will get in the Army, but maybe as I write you are a Buck private and I sympathize with your Squad leader. You will hate everything and every one for awhile, but after a time it will not be bad at all. Do not try to beat the army, you can't do it. Do not goldbrick and most important of all, dress carefully and stay as clean as possible and when an officer talks to you, be respectful. It will pay and I know. If you have an officer that is not qualified, do not show it. Remember he is an officer and that is your law. Do not talk much and never, never talk back to anyone no matter how dumb you may think he is. If you do these things you will get along fine and if you don't you will pay for it. Just because you see someone getting away with something, don't try it yourself. In order to be happy in the Army requires a state of mind. Remember this—anybody can be a good soldier part of the time, you be a good soldier all of the time. Well, it is about time for me to go over and get the Spam. I do not know how it will be fixed. We even have it in soup. I was an enlisted man for 14 months and you see I have seen things from both sides. The above advice is good and please keep it in mind at all times. After dinner I shall write some more.

Well, I am back at it again, it is now 1445. I have been to a meeting and have a whole page full of notes, mostly complaints about the food. Tonight I will go up town and visit my friends.

I go to see them every Wednesday night. They called me

up at noon and said to be sure and come early and have supper with them. The old man and myself will have a game of chess and this is a deciding game. We are 7 and 7 at present. I'll bet you didn't know that I know how to play chess. I learned how when I was in the hospital in Africa. It is a good game and I wish I had learned how to play sooner.

The sun is still shining and it is reasonably warm outside. I sure hope it warms up soon as I will be out in the open all next week. I sure do dread that. It is just too damn cold. There are a lot of things I would like to tell you about, but you would not understand them. They are mostly about the war and when I start to thinking about them, I get mad. I just took time and lit up a good cigar. The last box Papa sent me were Phillies and they sure are good.

You should see the stack of mail I have. I keep all of my letters that I have had since I have been away. The V-mail I have made into a book with a binder on it. The other mail I have in a box. All of the pictures I have in one large frame. I sure wish I had the presence of mind enough to have had pictures made of everyone and a case to carry them in before I left the states. The ones I have are a great comfort to me. I never cared much for pictures before.

One more little bit of advice. Have a large allotment made out. That is the best way of sending money home. Then it will go home every month and if you send it home yourself, you will stand to lose. I am going to stop soon as I have some work to do that I have been putting off all day. Tomorrow I think I will write Papa. He has been very good about writing to me. It is hard for me to write as I do not have anything to write about. I could tell you something about London, but it did not interest me and I do not believe it would interest you. Jerry pulled a few good raids while I was there, but that was old stuff to me. I saw a lot of places that I had read about. London is a big city but very much like any other big city. The war has had a strong effect on the people here. They have changed their ways plenty. Most of them have become used to the way things are and get along alright. It is considered alright for a married woman to go out with someone else. I know that for a fact. We call them 8th Army Widows. They have become used to the crowded conditions and the black-outs. There have been black-outs over here for a long time. You can walk along a dark street over here with a flashlight and see all kinds of strange things. I think most of these people are enjoying the war. That is what I hate about this damn thing. I went to see a show last night, "The Adventures of Robin Hood." By the way, I have been in Sherwood Forest. Well, Dink, write when you can keep me posted on what is happening. I am going to stop now and go to work.

Your brother,

Howard

We were used to seeing her around town this time of year—Miss Winnie Sledge, official family photographer from Shady Rest. Her car was not only loaded with her equipment, but she brought the striped-chintz, blonde, rectangle piano stool she posed everybody on from age two on up. It was always the classic pose, one knee folded under you as you sat, the other, scraped or not, dangling as the focal point of every picture. The younger ones, babies like Mary Howard, she put in any overstuffed living room chair with her quilted satin blanket covering the back. Every parlor had these pictures, just alike, and these were the kind we sent to Uncle Howard awhile back.

May 8th, 1944

England

Dear Dad,

This past week has brought me many letters. It is good to hear from home. I often wonder just what things are like at home. You cannot know what five years of total war has done to the people and the country here.

Before I go any further with this, there is a small matter I must tell you about. Day before yesterday, I cashed three checks for one hundred dollars each and one for eighty dollars. These checks were for cash and wish you would see that they are honored at the bank. I believe that my balance can stand it, but I am not sure. Please make the necessary arrangements as soon as you get this letter. You may wonder what I am doing with the money. I am having a good time with it. Money is cheap here. A man can go into a hotel bar and easily drink $40.00 worth of very poor drinks. In the past month I have had several days off and I made the most of them. I am sure that you are sorry to hear this, but it is likely that my days are numbered and I am drawing to an inside straight, so I am taking everything I can with me. I may as well make the most of what little time I have. A room for the night is $20.00 and it takes $2.00 to get a good seat in a theater—only then if you are lucky. Please do not get the wrong impression. I am not doing anything I am ashamed of or would not want my wife to know about. It is just that a few days away from camp cost like Hell, but I am an officer and I live in a glass house and it does one good to "get away from it all" for a little while.

The weather here is still cool. I have just taken off my overcoat. The days are over 19 hours long and are getting longer everyday. Today is a beautiful day. I should like to take a long walk with Dink, say from the brickyard up to the old, iron bridge and kind of talk things over. This world is kind of reeling under me and I am all mixed up. I no longer know what to believe in and I do not trust anything. I have seen too much and am afraid of what I shall see. I know it is coming and I shall be there—with men. Many men may die at my orders. That is my worry, but I did not intend to write all of this. I mainly wanted to tell you about the checks.

Tell Lib that she is next on my writing list and I shall write to her soon. Give the little blue-eyed girls my love and tell them what a beautiful old world it is that they live in. Later someone is going to have to tell their Uncle the same thing. Tell Ruthie I have not forgotten her.

I know that the place must be beautiful now—the white house and the green lawn. I bet the hedge needs trimming and the lawn needs mowing. If I were home I would trim the little bush by the kitchen window and give it up at that. Lib always said that that was my little bush.

Dad, I am sorry that I have caused you and the rest of my people at home so much worry since I have been away. Some of it was not my fault. The part about my being killed in action, I could not help, but soon the biggest part of it will come. Try and not worry for there is no good can come of worrying.

I shall very likely come out without a scratch. I shall try and let you know as soon as possible. I shall do my best because I do not want to sell out cheap. Please give my love to all and be sure and see about the checks. There won't be any more.

With love,
Howard

June 11, 1944

Dear Dad,

Once again I have my back against the sea. The last time I did not do so good, but maybe my luck will be better this time. It has been cold for the past three days and of course I am traveling light—one blanket and a raincoat. You would think that this time of year it would be hot, but it is a far cry from it. The days are very long, about 21 hours from light to dark.

I have had a ringside seat in what is called the greatest show on earth. I would gladly exchange it for a lesser one. I am very tired of big shows. Yesterday and the day before it rained ice water and I cursed whatever God there may be for sending me out in it. I sure do hate cold weather. The weather gives us fellas in the infantry a Hell of a beating. The enemy isn't enough, we have to fight the weather, too. When this war is over, I swear that I shall never be cold again. I do not know why I am writing at all for it is hard to find anything pleasant to say in my present surroundings. My blood really must be thin because I stay cold all the time and other people don't seem to mind it so much. I think that is one reason I hate Yankees so much. It is not good to hate people, but Dad, my heart is full of it. You may not be able to understand that, but you have never slept in ice water. I shall write as often as possible, but don't expect much. Tell Mamie that the slide rule is a great source of amusement, and that I carry it in my pocket. I look to the East and wonder what is in store for me. I will see Berlin yet and may not be long doing it. Tell the kids hello and give my love to all.

Howard

June 11

Dear Dink,

   Well, Dink, the last few days have been full of things to forget. I do not know what to tell you. Somehow I feel lonesome and I guess I want to talk to someone, but I just don't know what to say. I could say a lot about the past days, but I don't want to do that. The weather is foul and cold as Hell. Have you ever heard of being between the devil and the deep blue sea? I have been in that position twice now. This damn letter writing is getting the best of me. What do you want to hear about? I censor hundreds of letters. I have read thousands since I have been over here and they all look silly to me. I may give up writing for good. Have you got my sling shot rubbers on the way yet? Get me some if you have to take a tire off of a car. Well, Dink, I can't keep my mind on what I am doing. I will try and do better next time. Please do not worry about me.

With love, Howard

July 24, 1944

Dear Dad,

It is now ebb tide in my life. Never before have I felt so low. I am sure that I can not last much longer. I have had my share of this thing and am not through yet. We have paid a heavy price. I do not know what the papers say, but as in Africa and Sicily, the 9th Division has done much of the hard work over here. I know that I should not write like this, but there is nothing else to say. It is too late for me to come home now. I know that I am a wretch and I am not sure I even want to come home. Please give my love to all and do not feel bad because I do not write more often. I am so sick of war that sometimes I feel that I am losing my mind. It has been very hard, but the damn thing cannot last forever—not for me, it can't. All of my friends are gone now. I am a stranger in my own battalion. I shall try and do better in my next letter. Tell the girls that I will bring them all a present soon and tell Lib to save me some pears.

Notwithstanding,

Howard

I can't remember a hotter summer. Maybe it was because all of us stayed outside in the cow pasture and chicken yard picking up sticks, old cans, and bottles, helping Daddy with an all-out sprucing up. I knew there was that threat of Daddy's call coming anytime now, and I think he wanted to leave things "hunky-dory," as he called it. He spent more time with us, and we stayed up a little later at night, all of us sitting on the porch. I overheard them discussing what to do about the dairy once he was drafted, and they talked about selling big cans of milk to a dairy in Tallahassee. Anyway, sometimes when the heat was unbearable in the bedroom, I would lie there on the porch swing turning my pillow over and over from one side to the other hunting for any patch of coolness, but I could not sleep.

All during those steamy months I wondered when Daddy's name would come up. Did they really draw names from a big goldfish bowl like they had in another war? Is that what was meant by "the luck of the draw"? Sally and Mary Jean had gone to work in tobacco. Mama said I was still needed at home and in the dairy—we had started to outgrow playing wedding anyhow. Ruthie and I filled our afternoons making doll clothes and taking care of Mary Howard. We should have been saving cigar boxes to be used for shadow boxes in Bible School, but instead we made doll beds out of them and used Mama's wooden spools for the bedposts.

Often I would go over to Aunt Mamie's and watch her put her hair up with a rat, a sausage of net filled with her mother's hair. It was a special treat for me to watch her there at her vanity table combing her own hair over that contraption and pinning it in place so that it formed a neat roll at the base of her neck. She would sometimes let me look through her sheet music: "Harbor Lights," "Stairway to Paradise," "Wedding Bells Are Breaking Up That Old Gang of Mine." I wanted to ask her if I could borrow some, but I remembered one time she had told me, "Sari,

I would trust you with my life, but I wouldn't give you a piece of paper to keep for me for even a little while."

August 5

Dear Howard,

    It has been a month today since you wrote me. So I am looking for a letter from you soon. You boys are going some over there and I know there is not time for letter writing. But the faster you go, the sooner it will be over. May it, please God come to an end soon. I do hope you are all safe and sound and somehow I feel you are. Look to the one and only who can keep you from harm and bring you home again soon. We are all well and getting on O.K. I miss you and am anxious about you and maybe Dink going soon, but this is my part. We have quite a lot of rain—just showers and it has helped with the heat.

Love,

Dad

5th July 1944

Some muddy place in France

Dear Dad,

    Once again we have counted our dead and gone into a rest area. We will be here only for a short time, but that is alright because we are not getting any rest anyway.

    Sherman was right. I feel almost like a stranger here because there are so many new faces. Most of the old men are gone. Of the men that came over with me, there are only a few left.

I am in good shape and do not have a single scratch.

Give my love to all,

Howard

P.S. I am beginning to wonder if I have a right to live.

AUGUST 30, 1944

CHARLES B. BRADFORD, JR.

RICHLAND, FLORIDA

THE XE-SECRETARY OF WAR DESIRES ME TO EXPRESS HIS DEEP REGRET THAT YOUR BROTHER FIRST LIEUTENANT WILLIAM H. BRADFORD WAS KILLED IN ACTION ON ELEVEN AUGUST IN FRANCE PERIOD LETTER FOLLOWS.

J A ULIO THE ADJUTANT GENERAL 1129 A

Mrs. Mable Miller
Havana, Florida

Somewhere in Germany
September 20, 1944

Dear Mrs. Miller:

Just received your letter the second of this month and have searched for the orderly that you mentioned in your letter but have not been able to secure his name as there is not one left in "B" company that knew him. It seems such a shame that your brother, Howard, had to be taken so near the end of the trial and I can't understand why I am still on the scene when so many better soldiers have made the supreme sacrifice. To that end McCauley has joined Howard since my last letter so you see the grim reaper has not been idle at all in this so very grim business of ours over here, Mrs. Miller.

I feel that I sort of know you and all the Bradford family as Howard seemed to love you all so very much and spoke constantly of all of you. He was so worried toward the end about his older brother who was sure to be drafted soon. We were being shelled all the time and we read each others mail to keep from going mad. There are times over here when men bare their souls as they would never to anyone in a life more remote from the sudden death that we experience almost daily. Our chaplain was killed along side of Howard as we lay under a truck to escape some German shelling. Howard never knew what hit him and died before we could get him to an aid station. He was in no pain and left this world as he wanted to, doing his duty looking after the needs of the men.

I regret that he didn't get his picture taken while we were on leave in London even though he had that thought in mind. It happened that the Germans started bombing raids on London again and most of the shops were closed during our ten day leave together. I wrote to our mutual friends in London, Captain and Mrs. Leonard Plugge, telling them of Howard's being taken and they were very sad and upset to hear the news as they were very fond of your brother also. I sent all of Howard's possessions to the Effects Q.M. at Kansas City so they ought to be forwarded to you before another month is over. In it are the math and poetry books that he loved so very much and his uniform which I thought you would want to have along with his watch and personal papers.

If I am spared, Mrs. Miller, I shall come down to Richland as soon as I get back to the states at which time the veil of censorship will be lifted from the world and I shall be able to go into greater detail.

Again let me express my regret over the loss of your heroic brother, my friend Lt. Howard Bradford, one of the best officers to ever serve in the 60th Infantry.

Sincerely, 1st Lt. Dennis Lowe

And so, Aunt Mamie wrote in the Thanksgiving Book that year:

Now we know what a price war really is! What a terrible price to pay for freedom! I fervently hope and pray that our terrific sacrifice together with the sacrifices of the thousands of others will not be in vain, but that our country will maintain its freedom and be a better place in which to live.

Our day was clear and good again, urging us together on the banks of the river for a full day of fellowship. Turkey was again on the menu after an absence of one year. In spite of food rationing we had a bountiful feast! Some of us gathered wild flowers, beautiful autumn leaves, and holly, heavy with its bright red berries, which we used with fruits in making a colorful centerpiece the entire length of the table.

After enjoying the delicious meal, pictures were made of the different groups, then we signed in this record. Including the faithful servant, Gadsie, there were twenty present. Most of us visited around the campfire enjoying fellowship with our family after an early supper.

I had met the train with Granddaddy when the trunk came, but wasn't allowed to be present when they opened it. It was to be years later when I would be privileged to read just a few lines from the letters there in the Thom McCan shoe box on the shelf in Granddaddy's closet next to his tobacco—his burial suit hanging nearby.

They had read his last letter aloud to us and decades later I remembered the echo of his last line:

P.S. I am beginning to wonder if I have a right to live.

A right to live, I thought. How he had lived on—not only by his memory kept alive by the $4.26 monthly insurance check we swapped back and forth as teenagers buying $2.98 Butler Easter shoes, $3.98 jeans, four yards of Dan River gingham, even graduation invitations, but also in every generation of kin who chose his name. Mainly, though, it was his beautiful words with his personal honor code embedded there in the phrases holding on and holding out against unbearable torment and despair.

His was a rare intelligence—a curiosity running from the whys and wherefores of everyday logic, common sense, and intuition to a self-study of poetry, the classics, and ancient history. In his time and for our time, the scholar became teacher as he left lines more moving than those he had learned to love and recite. He gave life itself his own examination.

His life still touches us like a small ripple in a river

started by a single splash of a thrown pebble, the skim of a dragonfly, spreading and widening until it reaches the banks. We will continue to talk of the weather. The seasons will come and go and we will welcome their change. That is certain. Some years will be the "year of the berry," others will be the "year of the bush," but the letters will capture like photographs those long-ago seasons of uncertainty with words that will remain a part of us and keep us forever looking to another season.

Howard is buried in a military cemetery, Brittany American Cemetery, St. James, France. Granddaddy lived to be 90 years old. The house, before it was sold in 1982, was the scene of its last reception when Dink and Lib celebrated their 50th wedding anniversary. They now live in a retirement community in Tallahassee, Florida.

Ruthie teaches math at a private school in Gadsden County, while Mary Howard is a special education teacher in Thomasville, Georgia, and organist for her church. Sari is, of course, the author of this book. All three sisters and Lib make floral arrangements for social events, just for fun.

About the Author

Elizabeth Shelfer Morgan grew up in Havana, Florida, during World War II. There she married her childhood sweetheart in 1958. In 1988 she graduated from Florida State University with a Bachelor of Arts degree in English. Upon the recommendation and encouragement of her faculty committee, her honors thesis was extended to become her first book, *Uncertain Seasons*. She and her husband, Mark, have four children and two grandchildren and reside in Tallahassee, Florida.